RATS
IN A
CAN

BY THOMAS KIM

Cover design: Karen Phillips
Interior design: Vanessa Perez

Disclaimer:
This submarine model and its functions are neither current nor applicable to undersea operations of present day, and do not disclose any secrets. Only officers had access to highly classified orders and plans. The submarine is described as a nebulous form. I will share some profound events from fifty years ago.

Names are changed to protect the innocent and the guilty. Remembering and writing about the past is a difficult task. This is my account of living under the ocean for nearly a year. Hopefully, my memory wasn't completely washed away during the ensuing years.

Occurrences and events are confined within that time only, including spe-cifics of crewmembers with whom I served. Any resemblance to people now living is purely coincidental, including actions, descriptions, and names. The story is based on real life experiences, including my observations, perceptions, and opinions.

DEDICATION ~

Best wishes to all the brave and committed submariners while on patrol for an undetermined length of time. I too... was one of you, spending many tours in the dark ocean abyss fifty-one years ago. Enjoy the ride and behave yourselves. My sincere thanks and gratitude, for your courage and sacrifices safeguarding the free world.

PREFACE ~

TO WRITE A STORY that happened fifty years ago is an immense undertaking. Who in their right mind would even attempt such a daunting task? Still, against all odds, I decided to take this journey, to pick through forgotten memories, like hitting the reset button of my former life as a much younger man.

I was twenty years old when I joined the Navy, full of energy and high spirits. Following boot camp, I signed up for submarine duty. Serving on a submarine was the attraction for volunteering and to experience something different.

The submarine stories I tell family and friends are intriguing to them; and they want to hear more. Their encouragement led me to write my undersea travels starting from the enlistment period through discharge. Sections of the story are obscure, dark, and darker. Satire and humor lighten the journey. Written as a guided tour you'll find it new and insightful as I did living it. And I replied to the most frequently asked question: **"What's it like down there?"**

We're like "rats in a can", feeding on each other to get the upper hand or for the sheer entertainment of it all. Our body count was approximately one hundred-forty shipmates. This story is based on only my perspective and observations. Each of us had our own views regarding the matter.

Thousands of submariners have temporarily disappeared without explanation due to the "secret mission status" enacted by ruling naval authority. That still occurs today. Alive and well, they make their way through the deep, dark, underwater abyss, surviving as best they can, while trapped in this unique and bizarre reality. This story focuses on human behaviors, observations, and interactions while held within confined spaces for a lengthy period of time, often during drills of wartime conditions. Stepping away to get a breath of fresh air, to clear your mind is not an option. Living like rats in a can, can be stifling as a crowded prison ground ready to burst at the seams. Submarine life is a mysterious maze, a convoluted journey for those who live it. In short, life down-under leaves a lot to be desired; and no way out. Accept it and hang easy.

These are my observations and experiences as I remember them, and far from any pleasure cruise. The story contains some coarse language and salty descriptions. After all... we were sailors.

ACKNOWLEDGMENTS ~

A special thanks to several people for sharing their talents in making this book possible. To my editors: Zoe Keithley for her many years of excellence in writing and showing me the way, Ellen Karlstad for her relentless direction to "write it correctly." And to Chris Wenzl for lending unique insight to my story. Having "on the scene knowledge" as a former shipmate on the Grant. I relied on his creative frankness and proof reading skills to keep me on track 'til the end of the voyage. Thanks to Stephen Cook and Linda Weesner for sharing their professional guidance and assistance. Thanks to Ardene and Ted; dedicated readers to many impromptu sessions, expressing their candor and honest feedback. Special thanks to Karen Phillips for designing a great, eye-catching book cover. Thank you Vanessa Perez for a special book interior.

Congratulations to all for a job well done.

TK~

INTRODUCTION ~

After one patrol in a submarine, the first of many to follow was not considered my favorite endeavor by any means. Submarine life is an interesting study for just a short period of time. Learning all there is to know about this submersible, including the operations, standards, and procedures is a daunting task. It never lets up, leaving me with no rest nor peace of mind. It's devoid of any peace and quiet that you would expect down here while cruising in deep waters, and hard pressed to find any.

Any expectation of normalcy is buried within the confines of the underwater operations. This was our underwater world that had its hidden and nondescript facets. It's mired within a disruptive world which allows for no relief. What you see is what you get. Your first impression and your last will be short-lived as you observe and adapt to your surroundings. Annoying characteristics of man and machine make it that way. Moving through the ocean is basically calm and quiet; the internal features aboard are filled with both turbulence and subtle aggravations. Relaxation is mythical. That's why there's so much emphasis on sleeping down here, trying to "catch up." Dreaming is a good thing and therapeutic, when disappearing within your own mind is soothing. It brings out past pleasurable moments that you can rely on. Otherwise, you're caught in a state of undesirable thoughts, an accumulation of bad reminders of previous patrols. I know. I've experienced many of them.

Unfortunately, they're imbedded in your memory as bits and pieces, too many to recall in detail. Then, they seemingly break through the pores of your mind and seep into your conscious thoughts. There's no escaping this twist of reality. You can assume by now, the experience has left me with some scars over the past years. The nature of a submarine is a core of too much concentration; in contrast to its boring stagnation. There's no happy medium. It's either "balls to the wall" in crisis mode, or endless drills to fill the time.

There's no right or wrong about it while hovering in a state of mind, water, and space, waiting for the end to arrive. It seems as though you're in a prolonged time warp that drags on forever, with a far distant deadline in sight. You're slowly cruising through a twilight zone of neither black nor white, and attitudes of neither positive nor negative.

We're an underwater oddity traveling to nowhere, with a clock that was never set. I know it sounds like an unthinkable journey, but how else would you know unless you've been there. I'm assuming you're a rookie experiencing a blank mental vacuum about the possible end, but I'll fill you in with the "scoop." As I said, is it fiction or non-fiction, black or white? Could It be just a recollection of lot of brain washing...a lot of bunk of bent truth? Thinking back fifty years to recapture the moment, surely brings back possible inaccuracies to anyone's memory. There are a few blank spots in mine, but I'll explain the past the best I can in relating this story.

TIME AT SEA ~

Reflecting on decades past, time at sea was not agreeable with me. Submarine time was not the best kind ever spent. Time spent down here has a way of stretching out that seems never ending. If you've thought about it, we're like rats in a can. We're submerged underwater for months at a time, and hidden away from everything, including the seagulls flying above...out of sight, out of mind. It's the final act of disappearing. We're gone baby gone!...like we never existed. This can be interpreted as "a live burial at sea." The concept is a far cry from normalcy to say the least. Who would want to do this anyway? Sub sailors ought to be considered a bit mentally altered for volunteering for this type of duty under these conditions. In my case, I served for four years and didn't ship over in extending my enlistment. I got tired of being a participant in "a playground for grown men." Sanity finally caught up with me and pointed the way out.

During my "off" period, there was contrast in the side of life I missed everyday while at sea: Life in paradise that is more engaging, having sunrises and sunsets, enjoying tropical breezes while sitting on the lanai with my feet propped up, meeting women in great abundance, all while making new friends...Instead, I am stuck down here coping with the numbness of repetitive stagnation. Maybe the two months or longer will pass by quickly. My hunch says time will drag by slowly. It always has. This is the regrettable part of volunteering for sub duty. I just got here, but I need to get back to my other life, continuing where I left off...enjoying the simplicity of doing nothing, if that's what I choose. I miss my quiet time.

I require some sunshine on my body and sand beneath my feet where I can taste the salt air and hear the waves running across the beach and washing sand from under my feet. I can feel the arches being carved under each foot as I sink into the wet sand. I'll need to revisit the experience in my next dream. Dreaming is good...keeps me in touch with past pleasures of my other life.

I'm better connected with people back there, than I am out here. I don't particularly like living with other sailors, especially in tight quarters. It seems strange, but that's the way it is with a coping mechanism in place. When I'm back there in Hawaii, I'm free from rules and regulations. I'm more casual, more likable, more friendly and open. On the beach, I can be whoever I want to be. I'm just another beach bum. Someone else other than a sailor. I like it that way. I'm a clean slate without any labels. I'm just another local guy living in Waikiki. I can stretch out with more elbow room to move about. Time is on my side. I'm relaxed and having fun. When I'm out to sea, I can't wait to get back, so I can fulfill my other neglected pleasures of life.

Snap out of it. Like a slap in the face; I'm awake now, mysteriously transported, and now sitting at the helm...the brain fog is lifting. My day dream has come to an abrupt end as we rise to periscope depth. I'm no longer sitting at my favorite bar with a gin and tonic in hand. Both of my mitts are wrapped around the steering wheel of the fairwater planes. I'm working the steering and depth control, while keeping the boat at ordered depth and on the proper angle of turning to save our floating antenna. I'm back, sitting at the Helm. What the fuck, over!? Where am I? I need to get back to my daydream. As I said, "dreaming is good." I'm better connected with people back there than I am out here...even in my dreams."

JOINING UP ~

The year was 1965 and the Vietnam war was still exploding with expansion. Draft notices were sent out everywhere to replace the thirty thousand soldiers who were killed over the past years. Time was running out, and with my back against the wall, I decided to join the Navy my way to keep from getting killed in Vietnam. It was probably one of the smartest moves of self preservation I ever made. Soldiers were being killed at an alarming rate. Many of my friends were drafted, never to be heard from again. Death is final and there seemed to be no end to the slaughter. My high school friend, who lived down the street, was killed in action. His name was Jim Kelly, a Marine. He was a fast track star in high school. Nevertheless, he was struck down by a speeding bullet that took his life. Life is too short to end so quickly; and I didn't want to end up in his boots. My instinct told me I would be joining the death squad if I got drafted. This was the motivation to avoid going there. I passed my Army physical examination which placed me fit for duty. Waiting for my turn, it was just a matter of time before getting the call to report. Some draftees were dodging the war by getting married or running off to Canada. Instead of waiting for the draft to grab me, I quietly slipped into the navy.

Following U.S. Naval bootcamp at San Diego, I was transferred to submarine school located cross country at New London, Connecticut. Why I chose submarines is still a mystery to me. Maybe, it was a good idea at the time; and disappearing underwater would be another layer of escaping certain death, unless of course we sink. On subs it's all or none.

BOOTCAMP ~

My memory of bootcamp in San Diego was short and uninspiring, although the weather was the best, sunny and mild. If you squinted your eyes, you could be transported anywhere else on vacation, and with eyes wide open, it definitely wasn't here. The calm California climate was ruined by the reality of the bootcamp melee. Grinder duty, (marching in formations every day across the hot tarmac for two months), was the worst of the many parts of training. Our leader of Company 381 was Pappy Corcoran. He was a thirty year veteran, a Master Chief Petty Officer, and Boatswain Mate, who was well respected by his peers. He gave us serious lectures each morning as we stood at attention at the foot of our bunks, and he almost never hard-assed us. He chose a leader from our company to be his designated co-drill Instructor (DI) and leader. The chosen DI was the tallest man in our company of 70 men. I was 20 years old, one of the oldest. The others were just teenagers. Our company was a cross section of men from every corner of the country. After eight weeks there, we were whipped into shape. Bootcamp makes or breaks the individual. It's amazing to take 70 young men from all walks of life, and then mold them into one. It took months to get through the relentless pounding of repetition to achieve this goal. But, perfection was achieved from the non-stop daily routines. Basic training went by quickly, like a flash in a pan. But, in retrospect, it painted a more thorough and comprehensive picture of what would soon follow.

The reality of bootcamp, viewed from an outside perspective, offered a much larger and more complex picture than that of a young recruit. It was the organization of shuttling and the integration of thousands of enlisted men on a massive scale through the U.S. Naval Training Center. We were being prepped for war, but we didn't know it at the time. We were just young, energetic grunts arriving from everywhere of the United States. We were definitely out of our league. It was out of our control. We'd been tossed into the demanding confines of bootcamp (more like a meat grinder). We didn't realize what was planned for us, nor the scope of the operations. Watching the news before signing up for this misadventure may have given us a clue. Best guess for the younger recruits was that we arrived to enter an advanced section of Boy Scout training. However, at the time, it came across as a mismanaged cluster-fuck. We didn't realize the seriousness of the situation. Brought together in this training facility we needed to be clothed, housed, fed, tested (vetted), sorted out, classified, and streamlined by mental and physical training. Every phase of activity was a compressed schedule of time and space to fall within the guidelines and deadlines of parameters set forth by the navy. We were then gobbled up and spit out in two months, same as expendable pawns on a chessboard. Discipline was embedded into us via the arduous process of training at a blistering pace. It was a case of, in with the new and out with the old. Shit rolls down hill and we were standing down hill in the middle of the bullseye.

I had my suspicions of what was coming, being the end product of this downhill calamity. We were just recruits in the thick of things. Time flew by as bootcamp became a microcosmic blur of activity centered around our "Company 381." At the beginning we were the loose ends with no direction, just a part of a giant disorganized existence. Towards the end, we came together as a unified group, as our training was intended. We were just a small speck of 70 guys wanting to become sailors. "Leave us alone, and get us the Hell out of here," were my thoughts. We were ready for the next level to come our way. "We're done! What more do you want from us?" was our parting voice. We endured the daily routine of being yelled at, coping with the open blisters on our feet, the grueling and exhausting pace of passing time, the hurry ups and waiting, along with the other assorted dregs that replaced our sorely missed lives before reporting to here. The raw treatment reminded me of hell week in a fraternity. I was getting burned out by the relentless routine, like a circle with no beginning or end. As time passed, the circle was looking more like a straight line, an end to the madness was in sight. A light at the end of the tunnel.

Bootcamp came to an end as we wiped the last of the sweat from our foreheads. I can recall standing in front of our barracks as our next assignments were read to us and transfer papers were handed out. We stood gathered outside the barracks, listening closely to hear if our dream sheet picks came through. The guy standing next to me was assigned to a frigate, the USS Davidson, located in Da Nang Harbor, Vietnam. He was informed that his ship was sunk by the enemy the day before. The laughter faded as the report was read aloud, so everyone could hear the bad news. Shock and trepidation swept over his face. It was a haunting reminder to everyone that this war was the real thing. The drumbeat of war was headed straight for us and he'd dodged his first bullet already.

Soon, we'll all be sent out to get our hands dirty. Now anything can happen. My dream sheet stated I was headed for submarine school, located on the East Coast. It was with uncertainty that I entered the uncharted waters of submarines. Maybe this decision was becoming a case of buyers remorse. Time will tell…it heals all wounds. I have nothing to worry about. Ahead is the chance to serve my country. An underwater adventure awaits me, out of sight, out of mind. I will be a forgotten volunteer….just another rat in a can.

REPORTING TO SUBMARINE SCHOOL ~

It was cold and dreary when I arrived at sub school. An freak winter storm blew in, marking the ground with snow and icy patches. The bitter winter remnants covered the long stretch of concrete steps leading up to the classrooms. The barracks were located at the top of a slippery trek. I began my climb, using a death grip on the icy hand rails, pulling myself to the top with my sea bag in tow, alternating with slipping feet and cussing all the way to the top. It was a long way up, passing classrooms as they appeared either side of the steep climb.

We finally got there and checked in. The barracks were already filled with earlier arrivals to sub school. Our class instructor made use of the waiting manpower until the start of the next class. He volunteered us for clearing snow from various parts of the base. "Who is this idiot that volunteered us behind our backs?" someone yelled. We were designated snow-slaves until the start of class. "No word on how many days of this snow clearing detail, just get started tomorrow morning."

We seemed out of place carrying our snow shovels around the base. Low rumbling complaints were heard from the group. Finally, an irritating voice muttered. "Well, I certainly didn't sign up for this shit." I noticed the office personnel gawking at us through the windows. We were on display, slinging goddamn snow into the truck. Still restless towards the end of the day, some of us called a cab and headed for the nearest bar in town. We needed to unwind, relax, and do something meaningful to lift our spirits. Drinking booze to excess had the merits of offering some relief on a late weekday afternoon. We were only there for a short while. Then, we headed back to the base. The following day, I returned on my own. I was searching for something more meaningful and worthwhile to fill my time. Determined, I stayed until I found it.

It was only a ten minute bus ride away over the Thames River that separated the sub base at Groton from New London, Connecticut. Winter was ending and this offered us a chance to get out and enjoy the milder weather. The bus dropped me off on Bank Street, which had meager offerings. I frequented Joe's Diner. A long time establishment often busy with military and civilians. It was the only hub of activity on the block with the exception of Mc Arthur's Pool Hall across the street. It offered me a game with which I was familiar. Both places became a refuge when I came into town. It was something affordable other than loitering. They kept me grounded nearby and close to the base. A few blocks down the street was the train station. A right turn put you on State Street. Two blocks farther on was a local beer bar. It was located mid-block, filled with local blue-collar patrons. These two streets were my salvation during my sub school days. It wasn't perfect, but it provided a place of interest away from the base. Even if it was only to glance at the local newspaper while enjoying a hot cup of coffee. The change of scenery was just a fine offering of relaxation.

Life in the barracks, especially the noise, was becoming to be overwhelming. Loud radio music, bragging sailors telling endless stories of their past lives, along with the clouds of cigarette smoke drifting everywhere, gave me every reason to leave and seek a place of solitude. The atmosphere was an overkill of the wrong distractions for me to hang around. My senses were getting burned-out. Being surrounded in a place of peace and quiet is what I thought a barracks should be. But then it dawned on me, life under the sea, existing like "rats in a can" could even be worse. Whatever happens, I'll go with the flow and prepare myself for a considerable attitude adjustment.

GETTING AWAY ~

The cost of a cab ride off the base, even for a short distant, would throw my budget into the red. So, I caught the local bus instead. My first stop was returning to Joe's Diner. It was the only convenient coffee shop on Bank Street located near the bus stop. There was always an empty seat waiting for me at the end of the long service counter. Taking a seat there was handy for getting in and out of the busy place. Today, I was just in for a cup of coffee and looking forward to a quiet chat across the counter with my favorite waitress. She's the one wearing the light blue apron. Suzy was a short and spirited blond, somewhat older than me, and that was just fine. We bonded with each other over the next two weeks, including an unexpected fling. This morning, the counter was her service area. I caught her attention…"Hi, Swabbie! What can I do for you?," she said with a smile, passing me loaded with breakfast platters shingled up her arm. The morning rush was cranked up full speed, too busy for her to stop and chat. Maybe later, "I'll return when the rush was over."

"I'm off tomorrow," she said, and I showed up at her place unannounced, as I'd done before. There was no phone in her apartment for making a courtesy call before showing up at the door. This time was different…and a big mistake. She lived in a small upstairs studio apartment around the corner from the train station, and within walking distance to the diner. I arrived and knocked several times with no answer, only to discover that I was locked out. I later learned she was in there with her boyfriend who'd just returned from sea. She'd conveniently neglected to mention this other relationship. He was a secret and, unbeknownst to me, I was getting two timed by this innocent looking blond. The sudden change of events led me to step aside, as our brief fling fizzled away as quickly as it had begun. I became a third person in a relationship that was meant for two. I still patronized the diner, but the service wasn't as personal as before. Such a shame, no more desserts for me. The "blond-ala-mode" was no longer on the menu. The experience exemplifies the adage: "a girl in every port."

Loitering through town, I made my way back over to Mc Arthurs' pool hall and got engaged in another blistering nine ball shoot out. The eighteen year old kid was running the tables again. He always ran the tables because he was such an exceptional pool player. He was a staple of the place, and a serious contender to anyone who challenged him. The talented high school kid played like a pro. But did he know it? He was just playing for gas money, or so he said. Nonetheless, I couldn't beat him. I had sharpened my pool shooting skills while in college, but apparently not enough as I was no match for the kid. He was always winning my two dollar bets. During a break, I went next door to the Salvation Army and scarfed down two dollars worth of free coffee and donuts to get even with my loss. The kid clobbered me twenty times during sub school. I can barely remember beating him twice during our long shootouts. He was a smooth player and his shooting skills were like fine poetry, very polished. Leaving the cue ball only 4 to 6 inches from his next shot told the story. Sometimes he would even use two rails to pull off his magic.

He demonstrated magical brake control attached to the cue ball and with "the proper amount of english," to steer it with amazing accuracy. Pete was his name, ruler of the game, with a hidden talent. Dead-eye Dick may have been a better one. My brief encounter with this sharp-shooter, and getting hustled by this high school youngster, taught me a lesson in humility. Shooting against my opponent was an opportunity to observe his skills close up, and to pick up on a tip or two. I wasn't alone in my struggles to win a game. He beat everyone. That pocket full of greenbacks flashed as he bent over for his next shot. It wasn't all from two dollar bets. Chalking up that cue stick was an essential part of my game and I was glad to be grounded to something familiar.

Breaking that tightly racked triangle of balls was a flashback to my college days. Hearing that sharp crack of the break, then watching those colorful spheres scatter across the green felt was an old thrill coming back, like watching a kaleidoscope of angry buzzing bees moving at warp speed. Like a quick smack in the face, my memory was transported back home. Finally, awakening to something good. I spent many hours attached to that cue stick. My losses grew into gains in more ways than one. I knew that learning a skill in the navy would eventually happen, but I didn't realize it would be something from the past. I definitely saw an an improvement to my game while playing the kid hustler.

The offering of fifteen cent beer became a favorite of mine. It was my twenty-first birthday and I sucked down many. After pushing back the "State Street" bar stool after hours of imbibing cheap beer, I caught myself running down the street. I was running against my self, and survived. Feeling no pain with the cold air hitting my face, I ran as fast as I did while in college and grateful that I didn't collapse into the night streets. The beer buzz helped me with my balance and kept me upright during the night sprint. Spending my last four dollars on fifteen cent beer, it was a deal that I couldn't pass up. There was one other stop and that was the Salvation Army. Located next to the pool hall, it was open all night offering free snacks and coffee to anyone who wandered in from the cold. It became a regular "Palace" of salvation for me.

The pay of a navy sailor wasn't much back then. In some cases, starting pay was $108.00 per month, maybe a little more. Today's veterans begging on street corners, make better dough. Was this my future? Could I see myself standing on the corner rattling a tin can? Sometimes I would consider myself a straggler or drifter, being almost broke most of the time. It was an easy fit. Wearing my street clothes I blended in well with others. In those days people weren't labeled homeless, as they are today. They were just bums, hobos, or drifters. Maybe here on the east coast, they were called something else. For personal reasons, wearing my uniform outside the base was not an option. I didn't like people staring. When the night was over, I was grateful to have my navy bunk waiting for me. Sometimes in the late evening, I was the only person taking a cold and lonely bus ride back to the base. The guard at the front gate waved us in and I was dropped off not far from the barracks. Shuffling my way back, I hit the rack. Monday morning comes early and it's back to class.

IN THE CLASSROOM ~

We studied different classes of submarines. It was the Skipjack. A Nuclear Fast Attack classification that we concentrated on and studied in detail. We toured a vintage sub (boat) that was moored as part of the class and gained some insight into the learning process. My recollection of submarines was, that it was brutally difficult to learn. Too much to study with too little time, including too many parts and procedures to remember. At first everything looked the same in each compartment. It was cluttering the mind. It all boiled down to life and death situations while serving as a crew member aboard a nuclear submarine. No breaks for the fledgling students. Your mind is in constant flux. You're reviewing things that you are required to remember, and can't afford to forget. If you get too comfortable, it will come back to bite you in the ass. It is a constant mental grind with no rest for the weary, as I learned about these submersibles for the next several weeks. I was here for the so-called brain washing process and the washing went well. The more I learned, the more I regretted being here, and my classmates felt the same. I could tell from the moans and groans in the classroom. We proceeded to learn about submarine functions: All the internal working parts, compartmentation, safety procedures, and most importantly, damage control. We as students questioned whether or not our instructor was capable of relating all that information to us. He was quite a dumbfounded curiosity with other distractions that occupied his mind. The situation just needed some time, both for adjustments regarding the tough curriculum, and for the instructor to get squared away.

We were seated for our morning class to start at 8am sharp. Where was our class instructor? He abruptly entered through the side door of the classroom followed by a loud bang as he slammed down his books to announce his arrival. We "snapped to," as he caught us by surprise. Then, he showered us with a disgusting beer belch to capture our attention. He lacked in personal appearance. Very rough around the edges and looked as though he'd slept under his truck the night before. Hair not combed and face unshaven. And he started muttering something, that he was not quite prepared. There were no cuss words yet rolling out from his mouth and he seemed irritated that he was forced to show up for class this morning. He finally spoke, and introduced himself as the substitute class instructor. He was a real piece of work with his shirt half tucked in and far from making any current fashion statement.

The last time he looked in a mirror was long ago. His flamboyant personality wasn't his high point and didn't give us much encouragement for being here. His name was "Mitchell," and if I remember correctly, he brought his Napoleon complex with him. If he'd stood on a box during the lecture, he could garner some respect from his students. A nickname of "Shorty" would have been a better fit for him. He stepped outside while lighting up to take his smoke break. A cloud of white smoke followed him, hiding his face. He was standing in his smoking spot, marked with crushed cigarette butts covering the ground where he stood. Between the puffing and his coughing for the next twenty minutes, he used his cigarette butts for lighting the next one. The sure sign of a veteran chain smoker. At that time, he sent someone to fetch his coffee thermos from his truck. Looking down at the pile of the smoked butts surrounding his feet, I thought of saying, "that combination will stunt your growth...Shorty." It was just a thought as I walked by him to go back inside.

Our instructor was a first class blowhard sporting blood shot eyes. He was reminiscent of an old crusty version of the late actor "James

Cagney." Lecturing us with a raised voice, and pointing his finger towards us was supposed to mean something. Seated in front of him, we could clearly hear him, while his dragon breath cut through the frosty morning air. A handful of breath mints would have been useful in our defense. He was a demanding grouch and didn't receive much attention from his students. We didn't like him. He rubbed us the wrong way from the very beginning. This left us feeling that he was out for himself. His focus was somewhere else. This allowed ours to drift elsewhere too.

One morning his buddy showed up in our classroom to sell a new item he was hawking. Using high pressure sales tactics, he was selling his collapsable, cloth sided, plaid patterned, carry case. It was certainly ugly. Mitchell stood off to the side facing the class, glaring at us. He had a faint smile on his face as his friend bragged about his wonderful junkie case. It was "handy for carrying a case of beer for traveling," and "it would fit right in there," he exclaimed! It was such a stupid idea. Once assembled during the demonstration, the plastic handle was so stretched out, I thought it would snap right off.

Walking about carrying a heavy case of canned beer was his sad sales point. It was five bucks, with no takers from our class. Most likely, he got stuck with a shitload that he bought in Japan. Mitchell was embarrassed that his students didn't come through for his friend. I had a gut feeling he was going to make it even tougher on us students for the remainder of the class. It took a few days, but we all settled in and got along better. As time passed, he gradually cleaned up his act. I couldn't wait to get out of there in order to move on with the next stage of my life. So far, we weren't too impressed with submarine school. There was a certain lack of professionalism that I thought would be here, sort of center-stage, but, in fact, was missing. There was nothing that rubbed off on us, at least not from him, thank god.

Getting hustled for five-bucks was the main theme as a take-away from his class. It was a sore sticking point that eroded any seriousness in learning anything of submarines and submariners. The course should have covered a subject with at least a hint of an inspirational lecture such qualities as pride of service, the chosen few, exemplary men of the "Silent Service." Something other than beer belching and a snapshot of his personal grooming techniques. These important characteristics were missing throughout the course. It would have been useful in reshaping our attitude, thinking, and commitment.... certainly mine.

DAMAGE CONTROL ~

Damage control in a submarine is an important life saving subject. Quick timing and using extreme efforts for any situation involving flooding emergencies or fire requires immediate action by the crew. It means all hands on deck to handle the emergency shipboard crisis. Damage control is a section intensely studied, because nothing else matters when it comes to life and death situations. It's all about knocking on death's door. Plugging a leak in a tank, stopping a leaky valve, or handling a gushing opening is all about damage control. It's a simple concept. Your sub is underwater. Stop the leak before you drown!

Midway through sub school, our next task was to participate in a flooding scenario. We were tested at the damage control building. The task was to be held there, and we hiked over. Our class was divided into small groups following a short lecture. We were issued our damage control bags filled with the hand tools necessary to stop flooding situations. We laddered down into a large pit that seemed twenty feet across, maybe larger. The pit was a maze of tanks, lines and valves, randomly connected to each other, or not. We were looking at puzzling piping with mind boggling configurations. At first glance, it didn't make sense. I was thinking "Who was the mindless drone that put this together?" Then I realized, "It was set up for drowning us, like rats." The ground of the flooding pit was wet from smelly sea water of the previous flooding scenarios. I suspected the worse to come, as it was a do or die situation for us. We couldn't afford to panic.

Suddenly, water came crashing into the pit. Copious amounts of freezing salt water attacked us from all directions, like the spray of open fire hydrants. Our panic buttons were pushed and there was no game plan to fall back to. The flow increased and the squealing noise intensified as the valves were opening faster. A quick decision was made to pair up to deal with the flooding. More freezing water from a high pressure spray opened up on us, hitting us head high. We were soaked and blinded from the cold salty onslaught. Our heads were held down to keep the water from blasting our faces. The noise was deafening as salt water filled our ears, noses, and eyes. Our hands became frozen from the cold. Overwhelmed from the cold water shock, it was scary and unnerving. Like drowning rats, we frantically worked to stop the leaks, yelling at each other to get it done. The pit was filling up fast. Within a few minutes, the rush of water finally slowed to a trickle, as the waterline rose to our knees. The teams that didn't beat the clock had to repeat the task as punishment. Each flooding scenario was set up differently to trick the next group. The co-operative scramble was a cohesive exercise to demonstrate teamwork in a panic-filled situation. Everybody eventually passed. When the exercise ended, we poured out the water from our tool bags and boots. Totally spent, we were completely wrung out, exhausted as a tailpipe falling off a car.

WEEKENDS AT NYC ~

I usually travelled out of town with a friend from the base. This time, I caught the train to visit New York City by myself. If you traveled over the weekend wearing your navy uniform, the ticket was only $6.50 round trip. It was much cheaper for me than paying full price. The only time I was in uniform was to buy that discounted ticket. I didn't consider it safe wearing a uniform in New York City. I carried my bag with civvies in it. Changing clothes in the train's restroom was very challenging. It was just a little bigger than restrooms on today's passenger planes. Getting thrashed around by the train's movement while switching clothes became a problem, especially hopping around, aiming for the right or left pant leg. Changing required all the body co-ordination and balance I could muster-up while ricocheting off the walls in the tiny space. And all the while, keeping myself from falling in the toilet. As a matter of fact, I mentally drew a line of de-marcation, separating the filthy toilet side, from the other half of the floor. The cleaner half was where I wanted to be standing. Cussing un-der my breath, it made me think twice about buying a full-price ticket next time. But, I still couldn't afford it with my financial situation. It's amazing what I put myself through, just to save a few bucks.

The money from a sailor's paycheck was rationed until the follow-ing payday. Being stuck at the base mirrored a welfare case. I'd already experienced this way of life, having been raised on the edge of poor. Three meals a day and a warm bed at night was the same for us. It was room and board, navy style. It seemed to be a bare-bones minimum standard of existence. Life had to offer more than this. Up to this point, if there was any elite distinction or top drawer treatment within the submarine service, it must be reserved for officers only. That didn't exist here. This school was filled with enlisted grunts only. But I thought, sub sailors, even the enlisted, would receive better treatment and better ac-commodations than what I have experienced so far. I must have painted the wrong picture in my mind when I signed up to volunteer.

I needed a cure to break away from a boring way of life on the base. A need to do something drastic for a change was becoming a pri-ority. An unchartered trip to New York City and getting lost among the skyscrapers to fill the time of a Saturday afternoon was the an-swer. The challenge was to do it with forty bucks in my pocket. Once leaving Grand Central Station, it seemed as though I had to settle for a self-guided walking tour for the day. I strolled many miles with little money in my pocket. I was soon lost in the midst of high rise buildings with twenty foot wide sidewalks bustling with pedestrians and street noise. Above it all was the sky, appearing as a thin blue line caught in the vanishing point of the high rise buildings. A block later

I came upon a hamburger shop. The tiny diner seemed out of place, yet it occupied a corner notch of the high rise office building. The aroma of fried onions piled against the window by the grill caught my attention. The smell of grilled burgers drifting across the sidewalk awakened my appetite. It reminded my stomach that I needed to stop here and fill up.

I went inside and feasted on the three for a quarter miniature burgers, a meal matching my pint-size budget. Such a bargain, and I didn't get sick eating the bite-size food. That was a good outcome from a risky stop. I mentally charted a course to Time Square, which I thought at the time was the center of the universe. I headed there after getting directions from a pointing street vendor. Each New York City block became a long daunting trek in itself. Hoofing it block after block, I arrived on the edge of Time Square.

I spotted a nearby go-go dance saloon that offered two dollar beers. Although offering expensive beverages, quenching my thirst was in need of immediate attention. Nothing else mattered at the time. The flashing neon sign said, "The Metropol Cafe." My first few steps inside appeared dark as a dungeon with blaring juke box music. I entered with a frown on my face, as my eyes adjusted from the outside glare. A long bar occupied the left side of the entry. I focused on two large ornate bird cages hanging from the illuminated ceiling. Inside the cages, were two scantily clad go-go dancers with long blond hair. Below were beer drinkers lined up at the bar, all guys. All were looking up, bobbing their heads to the music....yeah. I was one of them. I slowly nursed my beer to kill some time, to rest my eyes more than anything. My neck was getting strained staring up at the dancers. Soon after, I pulled out from the bar and retreated back to the streets. I needed to continue my trek, to continue getting lost in my surroundings.

It was another hour of brutal walking with sore feet before I absently stumbled across Greenwich Village while heading back to the train terminal. In the village, I was drawn to music spilling into the street. It was a cocktail lounge and I stopped in for a beer to quench my thirst. The bar was unexpectedly filled with young girls. At the time, drinking age in New York was 18 years old. I was surprised being the only guy in the room, and felt out of place. Thinking I was crashing a private party, I finished my beer and bolted out of there to hit the streets once again. The atmosphere inside had all the markings of one of those beatnik joint's that I'd heard about. All the girls were dancing with each other on the floor. There wasn't another guy in sight. I like the odds but not the looks.

I finally gave in and hailed a cab to carry my ass back to Grand Central. That was my first and only cab ride in the big city. Being a cab-fare rookie in New York, I stood outside the cab to pay for the ride, a big mistake. I handed the driver a twenty dollar bill, expecting ten dollars back in change. He hit the gas and was gone in a flash. I was left, standing there, empty handed. Luckily my arm was still in tact, and me with my toes nearly flattened. He stole a tip that wasn't meant to be. I was thankful my arm was still attached as the cab raced off, leaving me flat-footed.

TRAIN RIDE BACK ~

I observed the main floor of Grand Central Station was a bustling crowd of two hundred people or more, yet mildly crowded with rushing passengers. The ceiling was tall and I found myself gazing up at this echoing three story high monstrosity. Impressed by its marble grandeur, I headed down to the main floor. Dodging the maddening rush of people, I wove a safe pathway down. I barely avoided tripping on a lady changing her baby's diaper spread across the main floor. She had to be crazy I thought and desperate to be doing this, and seemingly not minding the risk of getting stepped on. But, this was New York City, anything happens here. Needing to take a squirt, I spotted the sign pointing to the men's room, so I headed in that direction. It was a long walk down the wide and stained marble stairs to a landing. Then with a right turn, there was still another flight down as I arrived.

I rushed in with my bladder nearly spilling over, with my eyes scanning side to side, searching for the urinals, only to find the sinks were missing too. I didn't see anything resembling the men's room. So, I made another lap across the floor and spotting nothing. " What the heck, was I in the ladies room?" That can't be, there are guys standing around. Then, I noticed individual stall handles slightly protruding out from the walls. Hidden in the outline of the wall was a bathroom stall door. It was a dollar to get in. Not again, I was bleeding money since I got here. "No more peeing for free?" When did this happen? I dug deep to find four quarters to get in. Even the men's room found a way to squeeze money from me. To my surprise, when I opened the door, there was a toilet, a sink, and cloth hand towels inside. Amazingly, there was a full size self contained bathroom waiting behind the door. The only thing that was missing was some elevator music. I wanted to get every bit of my dollar's worth that I could. A minute passed when I heard thumps at the door. When I looked, I saw eye balls lined up at the door's-crack, staring in at me. I yelled "Get out of here you perverts." Charging the door, while throwing my bag with a loud bang, they scattered into thin air. I chalked up the incident as another strange New York greeting.

During my time at sub school, I visited the Big Apple just a few times. Seeing the big city was better than being stuck at the base on the weekends with nothing to do. My last trip to New York City was New Year's eve. Joining the festivities, blending in with a large crowd at Time Square was what I had in mind. Once there, and finding myself sealed in with tens of thousands of people, it crossed my mind, "What do I do when I need to hit the head?" Finding out the hard way, the answer came too soon. I got hit with an emergency. Trapped and squeezed like wall to wall sardines as far as the eye could see, I bulldozed my way through the crowds. We were so tightly packed, I floated across ankles and feet, as mine barely touched the ground. There was a lot of bumping, shoving, and swearing. I found a shop that was still open away from the crowds. The store owner took mercy on me and unlocked the door to let me use the can. The night was still young but I decided to head back to the base. Many times I gave some serious consideration to catching the train that went north to Boston. It was about the same distance from the base but in the opposite direction. I never did. Today, I have my regrets of not going there.

Midway through the school session, my friend Wes invited me to NYC for the weekend with two of his buddies. I had to pass on the invite as I was clearly out financed. A shortage of money was the main issue why I passed on the invite. They wore their dress blues (gabardines). Their gabs were custom made in Japan. They really looked sharp. "Thanks, next time," I replied, as they departed for the weekend. They were booked into a top hotel somewhere in Manhattan. Wes told me a story that happened when they went to dinner. Dinner was the highlight of their trip. Dinner was at Dempsey's, a long established famous restaurant in New York City. Jack Dempsey was a world class boxer in his day, and this was his legacy restaurant. Without making any reservations, getting a table in the popular place became next to impossible. Finally, after waiting in the street for a lengthy time, they slipped the doorman a twenty-spot to enter the place. The maitre d' hustled them inside through the main dining room. Moving quickly so as not to be seen, they were seated in the back section (beyond the view of the main restaurant floor). Their regular customers would be aghast if the sailor's presence were known. It seemed to have worked, slipping the sailors through the main dining room without getting noticed. The quick move avoided catching the eyes of the regular dining guests. (Sailors wearing formal attire such as their dress blues, were still viewed as second class citizens). At the time, Manhattans' upper crust of snobby elite society set the standards for the top-trendy restaurants in the City.

Wes continued telling his story: "After settling into their booth, a few minutes passed until an elderly couple seated next to them started in. At least she did. And out from her mouth came a barrage of verbal comments of displeasure aimed towards the company of those dreaded sailors. Just the sight of the sailors pissed her off." Wes said, "The wife had a real mouth on her. She wouldn't let up," complaining non-stop to her husband. "The poor bastard just had to sit there and listen to her endless yakking, in her raised voice. 'What's the world coming to? Sailors invading our place. It's just terrible.' She continued, 'I'm so embarrassed, our evening is ruined. I hope no one we know sees us, seated with this riffraff. I'll complain to the management after dinner.'" Wes said she was on a endless rant becoming a real pain in the ass. "Her poor husband just sat there in silence. He didn't mutter a word. He tried to hide his head by burying his face in his hands. He kept saying, 'keep your voice down.'" Wes said, "We pretended to ig-nore her elevated, unprovoked comments, but our ears were burning from the barrage of verbal insults coming from behind us. So, we kept calm waiting for her to quit, hoping that she would run out of air, or her false teeth would get dislodged and fly out. We said nothing, and called the waiter over to order dinner. Red wine was a must with dinner. 'We'll need two bottles of Cabernet Sauvignon. But first, a few shots of Jack Daniels Whiskey and Johnnie Walker Scotch to calm our ears.' The glass of premium red wine was used as a chaser to wash down the shots of hearty booze." he said.

"Finally, the lady took a breather and sat there quietly. She prob-ably needed time to rest her long winded mouth. The mood settled back to normal so we could rest our ears. Dinner finally arrived for us, the food appeared outstanding. This was the reason why we came here. We anticipated coming here for dinner months ago. My buddy Sam ordered a huge NY steak, charred medium-rare. It was perfectly grilled with mushrooms on the side. We toasted to our newly found restaurant and started chowing down. Then, just after our first bite, the lady started in again. We tried to ignore her. More insulting com-ments were fired off in our direction."

"Finally, Sam threw down his napkin, 'Well, I've had enough of this bullshit,' obviously angered. Sam trimmed off the big strip of fat that runs along side the length of the steak. It was every bit of 6" long.

He stuffed the end of the swinging strip of fat into a nostril. It dangled down past his chin. 'This ought to get her attention.' Then he stood up and turned his attention to the booth behind them, and faced the complaining lady. Sam, leaned into her and bellowed, 'EXCUSE ME LADY, DO YOU HAVE A HANKIE, I NEED TO BLOW MY NOSE.' She was stunned in shock, a real jaw dropper. It seemed to work in getting that mouth of her's 'zipped shut' for the rest of the evening. Not another peep was heard...dead silence swept over the area. We finished our dinners in peace and quiet. So quiet...you could hear a mouse fart."

A NEW JERSEY VISIT ~

Midway through sub school, my friend Nick invited me to tag along to join in his family gathering in New Jersey. Nick was Polish through and through, and had never met this part of his Polish family until now. We were both strangers showing up at the house as invited guests. He was Polish, and my racial extraction was Korean with just a quarter Polish. Both of us being Polish was our connection. Nick was amazed that I was part Polish, and sometimes I was too. It was confusing to him, knowing that my last name was Kim. "How can that be?" he thought. The name of Kimkowski could be a better fit as a mixed name, giving some credit to my Polish side. With a last name of Kim, Nick would need to explain this to his family regarding my Polish bloodline and how that occurred. We traveled to New Jersey by Greyhound Bus, then transferred to a taxi to finish the trip. After a lengthy trip, we finally arrived at the address. I'll never forget the house. It was an average looking, two story brick home, situated by itself on a large lot. I can't remember seeing any other homes on the block. I assumed the family owned the entire block.

Located on the adjoining lot next to their house was a large pile of scrap metal. The giant pile dwarfed the size of the house. It was protected with a tall cyclone metal fence. Nick explained that this was his uncle's business. According to New Jersey standards, they were considered very well-off. This immediately changed my outlook about the people I was about to meet. If I remember correctly, we showed up wearing our white sailor uniforms. The family was expecting our arrival. They had planned the gathering in advance, to celebrate our visit. They gave us a warm and friendly greeting, as they invited us inside for introductions. Other friends of the family were also gathered there to greet us. I couldn't help but noticing Nicks' three younger lady-cousins as we were introduced. They were all attractive, nicely dressed for the occasion, in their early twenties with big smiles on their faces.

Unbeknownst to us, they were kissing cousins. They started with Nick, including some hugging. He was somewhat surprised and embarrassed but went along with the idea. Then, it was my turn, so I wasn't left out. Observing what was happening, I was ready for their friendliness. Once they started, they wouldn't leave me alone. It extended throughout the day, but I didn't mind. I went along with the Polish tradition. Maybe, it was breaking away from their loneliness and expressing some affection. As the day progressed, they kept up the pace, as if I was expected to select my favorite from the three of them. I was relieved that others were present in the room, otherwise I'd be in deep trouble wanting them all. Somehow, they thought we were military heroes. I didn't know what Nick whispered to them earlier, most likely, some heroic submarine stories involving us. Nick smiled and winked at me sending me a message as he leaned over and whispered in my ear, "have a great time...you Korean-Polack." The young ladies were silently coaxed to show their affection. I didn't care what took place, while I continued enjoying myself to say the least.

The father of the house insisted on getting us drunk, led us downstairs into the large, party size basement, his secret bar was tucked away in the dark corner of the room. He proudly unveiled it to us, as he flipped the lights on. He added some music and started mixing cocktails. There was plenty of liquor and mixes stocked in his bar inventory to go around. Anything we wanted was in his well stocked arsenal of liquid ammo. The father volunteered as the bartender for the day and it was a busy afternoon for him. He insisted pouring drinks for everyone, as guests lined up at the bar. He drank many of his mistakes that he purposely made for himself. Many times he had one in each hand.

Later that afternoon, the father continued bartending and was talking to his guests using the Polish vernacular. For the most part, the Polish articulation came out slurry and garbled. As he continued speaking, he was unknowingly destroying the last of of the Polish language in short order. I was dumbfounded by what he was saying. Just a guess, maybe so was he. I know. I've been there myself in an attempt to engage in conversation, while tripping over my inebriated words of wisdom. The father's comments blended with the rhythm of the music. As he continued talking, I smiled bobbing my head up and down, keeping with the beat, as if I understood every word he was saying. Not to be rude, I didn't understand a damn thing he was saying. But, it was not all a lost cause, a little pizazz was added to the foreign gibberish.

Meanwhile, upstairs his wife was preparing a bountiful spread of classic Polish dishes that was served buffet style. We were wined and dined all day long and into the early evening. By this time, we were three sheets to the wind, working on the forth, and feeling no pain. I certainly enjoyed the warm Polish hospitality that day.

During my sub school days, the visit to New Jersey and meet the Polish family was the best time ever. At the end of the day, we were sad to leave. I can't remember why we only went there once. But, If it was located any closer, it could have easily been a daily hang-out for me. It was a long good-bye that included more hugs and kisses. They asked us back at anytime. We enjoyed each other's company so much, I was nearly adopted as a missing Polish cousin to the family. Soon we were on the bus, returning to base. I slept most of the return trip back. It was the best Polish encounter that ever happened to me.

THE DREADED DIVING TANK ~

The purpose of the diving tank is for training navy divers. They are required to meet and maintain certain criteria for their certifications. The submariners are required to undergo tank training for other reasons. They must perform emergency evolutions, required actions while under stressful conditions, and perform them successfully within confined spaces. Tank training will help them fulfill the necessary requirements in surviving. Submariners must trust and follow proven procedures. Concerns of claustrophobia would certainly be addressed and detected during these training exercises. Sailors unable to successfully pass the minimum three tank ascents were cut from the submarine program.

Towards the end of the class, we each faced the dreaded three unassisted buoyant ascents. This was a constant worry during sub school. We gathered in groups, speculating about this journey with trepidation and concern. The day finally arrived. We each had to ascend through 50' of water using only a single breath of air. I thought this was impossible. I just had to trust what I was hearing...even from our flakey instructor. This was the same tank that was used for training navy divers. What could go wrong! Although the tank was filled with 100' of water, our class of 37 students started at the required 50' level. We did this maneuver twice with an air filled neck collar. The neck collar was added buoyancy for lift. Blowing the air from our lungs was necessary on the way to the surface to prevent air embolism, the bends. Our next evolution accent, we used a Steinke Hood, yelling Ho-Ho-Ho, all the way to the surface. The reason for expelling the compressed air from your lungs is to prevent injury to them. You must blow air all the way to the surface, using only a single breath of air. The navy diver will hold you in place until he sees air bubbles escaping from your mouth, then he'll release you. The three mandatory ascents will definitely separate the men from the boys. You're concerned about running out of air, but amazingly you don't.

The anticipation of the buoyant ascents was a worry to everyone leading up to this day. Groups of six to eight rode the elevator up. We were loaded into a small spherical pressure chamber after exiting the elevator. It looked like a space ship launch. Inside of the chamber there was a circular bench of wood and a steel door next to it that opened into the tank. We were tightly seated, jammed in a circle facing each other with knees and shoulders touching, like sardines squeezed in a tin. It was hot, very humid and difficult to breath. We were cramped in this position for at least thirty minutes being lectured. It seemed like hours. There was a small light on the overhead for illumination. We carefully listened to our diving instructor. It was important to follow exactly all the steps and procedures of what was to happen next. After all, we risked a chance of drowning in the tank. With this in mind, the physical discomfort we were experiencing disappeared. We sat there sweating, listening to his instructions. We had to maneuver from this chamber, into the diving tank while using exact precision of action, turning the body, and hand positioning. There was no room for error. Any sandbaggers among us, (those susceptible of having claustrophobia), would soon be spotted. The idea of not running out of air by blowing all the way to the surface was not setting well for any of us. Good luck to any claustrophobics hidden among us. Trusting the unknown is very nerve racking. We all knew thousands preceded us, and many would follow using the same technique and procedures.

LIFE IN THE FAST LANE ~

The waiting was over. Now it began. We put on our neck collars and the instructor filled them with air for buoyancy. The diving instructor flooded the chamber. Just our heads and top of the shoulders were above the waterline. Next, he opened a valve and screaming air shot into the remaining upper part of the chamber. The noise was deafening, just as he had warned us. The air pressure will plug your ears, and even burst your eardrums in some cases. A small trickle of blood coming from the ears would indicate that an eardrum was compromised. You need a two week healing period to retest at that later date. The air pressure in the chamber is necessary to equalize with the same pressure against the door in order for it to open. Equal pressures allow access into the flooded one-hundred foot vertical tank. Our test started at the fifty foot level. One by one, we each took our turn entering the tank using the prescribed method.

When it was my turn, I took a deep breath of air and ducked under the water, clearing the door opening. I slipped sideways into in the tank, an area of underwater suspension. Like a fish in a aquarium, looking up was bizarre. I saw the safety diver stationed outside the door. He held me in place as I assumed the correct position: Arms stretched over my head with hands pointing up and the thumbs interlocked. This acted as a rudder for steering upward. My feet were together with toes pointed down. The diver held me in place, then he let me go, but only after I started blowing. I watched the stream of bubbles leaving my mouth, heading for the surface. There were two safety divers stationed above me at different levels. They were to assist us in case of trouble. I saw the diver stationed by the diving bell. You would be assisted to the bell for air if you freaked out and needed emergency air, or freaked out and quit blowing. Air embolism occurs if you stop blowing and the expanding air in your lungs causes injury, or it can even kill.

The ride up was instantaneous, as if riding a lightening bolt to the surface. The stream of bubbles leaving my mouth were way beneath me. It took only seconds to move through the fifty feet of water. When I reached the surface, my body shot out of the water, clearing my ankles. Divers waiting on the top fished me out of the water. We repeated the same ride twice. The second time was fun. During this ascent, a diver came up from behind me. I didn't see him. He quickly spun me around to put me back on course and my legs flew apart. My left leg swept across his body accidentally kicking him in the balls. My foot was planted with unsuspected accuracy. It was purely accidental, but I thought I flunked the test. Afterwards, I had a smile on my face, realizing what I had done. Traveling to the surface was so fast, the white knuckle anticipation was a waste of time. The whole experience was a stroll in the park. In retrospect, it was just a matter of pushing aside your fear of the unknown.

Then, we made our final ascent wearing a Steinke Hood. The Steinke Hood was a buoyant vest made of pliable high-tech material, international orange in color. It was secured over our heads and had a window. The fit to the body was awkward but water tight. For all intents and purposes, the vest was the navy's last ditch attempt at offering some reassurance for survival while escaping from a sunken submarine. The truth of the matter is, getting your eardrums blown out in the pressure chamber during practice is one thing, but it cannot be compared to the real situation. In a true life scenario, the sub and the crew would be crushed like a bug from intense sea pressure, while sinking for miles. Oceans are deep and no one can survive "crush depth." "Crush depth" is a marker that is beyond a submarine's safe diving depths. Think about crushing an aluminum beer can with a clenched fist. It leaves dramatic results. Yikes!

At least thirty seven of us made three successful ascents each. It took all day to complete the testing. It was a pass-fail exercise. Thirty-seven passed from our class. When sub school was over we had a class photo taken together. I'm sure there was some kind of a celebration afterwards. I can't remember what it was, probably because it involved alcoholic beverages. We were now looking forward to moving on to our next assignment. I chose Boomers out of Pearl Harbor. First it was back to the sub barracks for another few days pending our transfer orders. Soon, I was on my way to a new duty station located in Paradise.

LEAVING SUB SCHOOL ~

The next thing you know, I left sub school and headed for my first assignment listed on my dream sheet. I requested FBM's (Fleet Ballistic Missile Submarines) out of Pearl Harbor. FBMs are nicknamed Boomers. Boomers carried an arsenal of sixteen nuclear Polaris missiles. That's how they got the name. I chose a West Coast sub base in order to be nearby my girl friend who flew for Western Airlines. Sharon was a new hire, and just graduated from stewardess school (their title back then). I met Sharon at City College in Sacramento. I spent more time shooting pool at B&A pool hall than I did with her. It was just before my first patrol when we finally got together. It was at the end of my first patrol from Guam when I received my "dear John" letter from her. She married a friend of mine back home. I was quite stunned reading the "bye-bye" letter. I was expecting something else, like how much she missed me would have been less painful. Instead, it was a real Boomer-bummer message. I assumed she had to move on with her life and sought better stability in a relationship. Ours had none of those characteristics. For the most part, long distant relationships really didn't work anyway. Statistics don't lie.

Marriage was a foreign subject to me. I back-peddled at the concept of marriage. I didn't realize she had such designs on me…but maybe, it just was not with me. We never discussed the subject. It never crossed my mind. It was tough enough taking care of myself. I wasn't prepared for any kind of commitment like that. Being apart most likely led to her decision and I was aware that long distant relationships failed most of the time. Being tied down with the navy and doubling up my obligations with marriage, just wasn't in the cards. That whole idea became a fading memory. Living a simple and carefree life was just beginning. That appealed to me. The other, not so much.

Besides, I was too young to do such a tragic thing to myself. Our lives were too separated and our goals seemed so far apart. I knew that divorce ran rampant in the navy. Divorce impacted FBM sailors more severely and more frequently than anywhere else in the navy. As an example, our sub alone produced nine divorces just after one patrol. My family back home, was already littered with several divorces. Many of the women in my family pulled the plug on their marriages for a variety of reasons. There was no reason for me to participate in our tragic family legacy. I had every reason for not joining their divorce syndication. Looking at a poor track record with my family history, and that of the submarine duty, spelled disaster regarding the "I do commitments." Besides, I had to live up to the sailor's motto "a girl in every port," or was it, "a girl after every patrol?" My intention was to stay in paradise and find out. I struggled to carve out a small retreat for myself. I wanted to stay there and explore it. Besides, Sharon was in good hands having chosen the right guy to marry. It was one less situation for a young 21 year old sailor to worry about. Anchors aweigh, me boys!

ARRIVING AT PEARL ~

I soon realized that life on the sub base at Pearl Harbor, was no better than the one I had left on the East Coast. The high humidity here was like taking a shower and never drying off, "like misting water to make it wetter." The only upside to living here would be nicer weather, surrounded in a tropical paradise, and beaches covered with skimpy bikinis drenched with suntanned curves. Basically speaking, what else would I need? The FBM base and barracks was located on Ford Island, a land mass in the middle of the harbor. One side was marked by several sunken battleships. It featured the Arizona Memorial, a shrine poised just under the water's surface. I passed by it every morning, using the available navy ferry as I headed to my assigned barracks. I looked back over my shoulder; and ten miles behind me was Waikiki. Everything I needed was there, not here. Ford Island was a big disappointment. It appeared to be desolate, marooned, too isolated, too commercial, and too military. There was absolutely nothing here for me. I learned that sub sailors were allowed to live off base. I thought I would give that a try.

Needing transportation to get me around, I bought an old 1950 black and white, 2 door Ford sedan. It still had a pulse. It started easily and ran forever. I didn't give it a name, but we easily bonded together during the many miles that I spent behind the wheel. It was riddled with rust and basically ugly overall, yet beautifully affordable. Parts were not as falling off, so it qualified as good, temporary transportation. It cost a $100. The old flathead v8 still sprang to life under the hood. It came with squealing brakes, which acted like a built-in horn warning the J-walkers to pick up the pace or die when they heard me coming. My daily goal was searching for an apartment until I found one. My beautiful car wasn't much, but together we could find what I needed. Living in Waikiki was the answer and it was only a short drive away. I made several trips shuttling back and forth, looking for a place on the beach. I needed to make a move away from the sub barracks. Why live anywhere else in this paradise. Ford Island was not the island I had in mind. As long as I wasn't at sea, I kept on searching to find somewhere better to call an island paradise.

During one of my many searches, I purposely veered off course taking a side trip to the older section of downtown Honolulu. Intrigued by many stories told by veteran sub sailors, my curiosity led me to visit the historical section of Chinatown for myself. I needed to cruise down the infamous "Hotel Street." It was the main street in Chinatown. The sailors called it "Shit Street." A fitting name, due to its rundown appearance and seedy reputation from yesteryear. I understood how it got its name just by taking a slow drive-by. I envisioned sailors from the past, coming here to get their tattoos, drinking excessively, getting rowdy, being chased by the shore patrol, and finding their favorite ladies of the night. Chinatown, Honolulu was a sailors' paradise for taking liberty before moving on to their next port. The area of commercial wooden buildings was a historical throwback to the early 1900's. They had definitely received their share of getting weathered, worn, and abused. It was ironic that my vintage, rust-stricken Ford jalopy blended in well with the surroundings. I made one stop to pay homage to the "Pantheon Bar." It was noted as being the oldest bar in Honolulu. At the time I visited, it was 88 years old.

The wooden relic was built in 1878 and became the Pantheon bar in 1911. It showed every bit of its age. The inside was worse than I expected. After entering, my eyes took a few seconds to adjust from the glare of the outside brightness. Inside was dark, dank, which appeared unkept, a raggedy refection of its eighty-eight years of age. The planked wooden floor creaked when I moved across to take a seat at a table. I caught myself staring at the back bar. I noticed it was moving and I hadn't had a drink yet. I rubbed my eyes for a better look. Then, I saw small gecko lizards running in and out of holes in the wall of the back bar. It was noon time and there were only a few patrons drinking at the time. I noticed an elderly Chinese woman standing at the end of the bar. I was thinking she was a regular customer, and maybe her age matched that of the place. She slowly shuffled her way over to my table to take my drink order. She stood out from the others in the room, wearing a brightly colored muumuu. When I looked up, her facial features caught me off guard. Her long grey hair partially covered her smiling face and I noticed that her teeth were missing along with her left eye. I caught myself staring at the deep crevasses crisscrossing her scared aging face and was taken aback from what I saw. She was quite a fright, but seemingly a nice lady when she spoke. The scotch and water arrived and I quickly finished it. I needed that drink to forget what I just saw. Uncomfortable sitting in the empty room and feeling out of place, I found myself in a rush to leave. I'd seen enough of the Pantheon.

I went out through the back exit looking to use the men's head. Immediately I was trapped, standing outside in a narrow, and partially blocked alleyway. There was a long metal trough to use as a urinal. It was a old aircraft fuel tank cut in half and bolted waist high to the exterior of the building. It was partially covered with a ratty, torn lean-to roof. Behind me, I was exposed to the world. There was an older two story rooming house with open windows looking down on me. It was so close, that if someone were to spit, it would hit me in the back of the head. There were clothes draped over the openings drying in the sun. You can see and the smell the cigarettes venting from the open windows. Thinking about where I was standing, I quickly changed my mind and retreated back inside. I didn't have to go that bad after all.

SEARCHING WAIKIKI ~

I continued my search in "Wai-khaki Beach." One afternoon I was running down leads to find a place to rent. At this point, I was parked to scout the territory on foot. It's such a small world. What are the odds of timing and being in the same location. From out of nowhere, appeared my cousin Steven. He was also roaming the beach area in Waikiki. We were family growing up in the same house in Sacramento. We were close and about the same age. Steven and his college buddy were already renting a place nearby. I temporarily moved in with them as I continued to hunt for my ideal beach apartment. Steve landed a scholarship to the University of Hawaii, which brought him to the Islands. He said he left the University at Santa Barbara for a better paying scholarship here. Such a lucky-smart guy. His plan was to move to Maui soon after college. His Santa Barbara friend who lived in Maui, was starting up a bicycle business. Steve was asked to join him in the business venture. Our time together was a brief visit, as we got caught up, filling in our time apart to present day.

It was getting late. I had to move on with my quest in finding a new place to live, as everyone was being shuffled about. Finally, my search landed me in a place across the street from the University of Hawaii. It was located in the Manoa Valley. Although it was outside of my comfort zone away from the beach, I anticipated my temporary digs to be very interesting. Living in the thick of things amidst the college co-eds, instead of sub sailors, was a change I was looking forward to. Surrounded with young ladies, instead of men, I couldn't ask for more.

Time was running short so I answered an ad in the local newspaper. I moved in with Charles Reyes and Ron Biffeti. I became the third roommate in an upstairs apartment. Moving in to occupy the extra bedroom was based on a temporary "move in situation," which was fine with them. The rent was cheap, $35 a month for my room. Charles and Ron were older graduate students attending the University of Hawaii. This was my first experience living with the scholarly types and I soon adjusted to the change. The three of us had different agendas of interests. They were home bodies, busy studying for the most part, and I was the loose end, always looking for something to occupy my time. Several young ladies were spread throughout our building that my roommates had already befriended. There was an open door policy at our apartment complex. Friendly neighbors could drop by to visit whenever they wanted. It was literally an open door policy. The door was always propped open. Easy access, even for the Gecko lizards to wander in. Everyone who lived in our building seemed to be closely connected to my roommates. I realized that the students in our building had already developed a close knit, family relationship, rather than just being acquaintances and friends. Many young ladies dropped in to strike up a conversation with the mature Chicago native, Ron Biffeti. They sought comfort with Ron for a variety of reasons. From class problems to personal problems, everything had solutions with Ron as their mentor.

Ron was forty years old and a veteran of many lifetime travels and experiences. That seemed to be the attraction for many of his female groupies. His maturity, small stature, Hawaiian akamai (island smarts) and his strong Chacago accent were magnetic draws that led to his popularity. Ron's expertise was journalism and he had a diverse tongue in foreign languages. He often communicated with Charles in the Filipino dialect. Several times I watched him pound out many paged reports without any errors or typos. He was a natural when using his vintage typewriter. He was aiming for a masters degree in journalism. Ron was a trusted gentleman around the young ladies in the building. He wore several different hats. Big brother, uncle, or a wise father figure to many of the young students who sought his mature advice and diverse savvy. Watching the master at work, I quietly observed his nonthreatening approach and his social mannerisms, as he casually tutored others in the building. I met many of his acquaintances. Living there was fun and a contrast to my other smorgasbord of unsophisticated sailors. I enjoyed being surrounded by higher forms of intelligence for a change. I appreciated living there under the circumstances, but, I was adrift and too far from where I needed to be. Once again, I focused my attention on finding my own place, closer to the beach, the center of activity. It didn't take long for me to cross paths with luck during my continued search. My rusty trusty Ford sedan led the way.

Driving through the streets of Waikiki, I soon located another possible contender to call home, when I happen to look up and there it appeared, staring me in the face. It was a "for rent" sign that grabbed my attention. I could have easily driven by and missed it. It was part of an old faded turquoise, two story, stucco apartment building, and home to sixteen units. I met with Betty, the landlady and owner. She seemed to be a nice lady during our brief conversation. The white Corvette convertible parked in a private spot out front, was hers. Betty was a middle aged lady who liked sailors and drove this classic sports car. She had style, answering the office door to greet me with a cocktail in one hand and a lit cigarette in the other. Her voice was moderately raspy from too much smoking over the years. She seemed financially comfortable. The rent money she brought in, was augmented by her late husband's pension. Betty was easy going. Nothing could be better. The only time we saw her was once a month to pay the rent. Finding this apartment was lucky and painless. Luck was on my side that fateful day. It was as if Betty knew I was coming and had saved it for me.

The apartment was the first one upstairs, #12. It was conveniently located only two blocks from the ocean and in the heart of Waikiki, a rare and tremendous find. I immediately started feeling better again. The amazing sunsets from the upstairs Lanai were almost enough to make me forget I was in the Navy. The monthly rent for the apartment seemed like a gift at only $150 a month. The reasonable rent was surprising and an unexpected bonus. It was such a surprise that I didn't have to barter for cheaper rent. Betty's late husband was a retired Chief Petty Officer. She passed on the "reasonable rent," as a way of giving a good deal to sailors in need.

The following day, I introduced Betty to Chris, a fellow ship-mate and friend. Then we headed upstairs to show the apartment again. It was clean, nice, and minimally furnished. We could care less, we'd landed in paradise! Betty held firm that rent was to be paid on time, and that she trusted sailors as being solid renters. She handed me a pen, and we signed the rental agreement. She politely and jokingly said with a smile, "keep the noise to a minimum and no wild parties...of course, unless I'm invited." We acknowledged her wishes as she was leaving. Later, we agreed that she was not to be invited to any of our parties. Betty had already seen too many parties. Those telltale years of partying were showing through her heavy facial makeup told us so.

OFFICER'S DISCORD ~

Aboard the Grant there was one mean spirited senior officer. He came across as having a chip on his shoulder. A hard-boiled exterior accompanied his angry demeanor. The crew dubbed him Mr. Happy. He was disliked by the majority of the crew. He didn't score many points because of his disapproval of a small group of non-qualified sailors living-off base, which included me. He purposely withheld, (not paying a single red cent) towards our various assistance housing allowance and other benefits, to which we were entitled. Nevertheless, it was used as some kind of a personal vendetta against us. He had hopes of financially breaking us to keep us from moving off base. It was meant to be some kind of hidden punishment. Receiving this extra pay was based solely on his discretion and approval. Many of us who were financially strapped by his decision, moved off-base anyway. In some cases, it was done just to piss him off. Our spirits were stronger than what we could afford. The action of the officer was confusing and inexplicable. The senior officer acted as if our pay was coming out of his own pocket and attempted to put a stop to our plan. Blame it on too much time at sea. Such things can influence people into making rash-selfish decisions. I concluded that he was just a miserable person who wanted to bring us all down to his level.

However, after some discussion with those in the know, we discovered that others on our boat and on other boats in the entire FBM fleet received this pay. But, we were excluded with no recourse of action. The off-base housing allowance pay, which it is now called BAH, is a substantial amount, sometimes matching or even exceeding the amount of a regular paycheck. The significance of the pay was like drawing a bonus. We drew no conclusion why we were exempt, other than the senior officer didn't like us. Maybe, our group strayed too far outside the pattern of normal, acceptable, military behavior. The most likely reason was that "His wife must have cut him off before going to sea, which put him in such an angry frame of mind." Whatever the reason, whispers from the Yeoman (office-secretary of the Grant) said he was aware of the rumors but couldn't clue us in any further. He knew, but couldn't say any more. It was an after the fact warning that he gave us, but still it offered no reason for cause of action. Not understanding the internal dynamics of this man's decision to do what he did will remain a mystery. Either way, qualified in subs or not qualified, it didn't matter, not receiving the nearly $6 to $7 grand in pay, over a two year period was a small fortune to each of us. It's amazing how Mr. Happy got away with controlling the purse strings and manipulating the pay schedules. My financial situation would have been totally reversed having received this money. This single event set into motion a lack of trust for this officer (officers). Getting cheated goes a long way by us not forgetting.

In spite of the many financial difficulties that confronted me, I still made it a priority to move to Waikiki, as quickly as possible. I was challenged to be living in the most expensive vacation areas in Hawaii. I moved there with limited funds just to prove that it could be done and survive. A new sailor checking aboard the Grant opting to live off-base must have set a bad tone with this officer. "New guys coming aboard weren't suppose to afford that." They probably thought I had another source of funds to afford living there, which wasn't the case at all. Perhaps, it was a matter of they just couldn't handle their jealousy.

"Wait until we go to sea, was the scuttlebutt" (rumors of what I heard). I believe someone at the top created a hidden agenda for us to be singled out for more untenable treatment. I learned from my own pipeline of information gathering, that I was correct. During that period, I unfairly received what I thought it to be more than my share of misfortune during the five patrols while serving on the Grant. Unbeknownst to me, I was placed on somebody's secret "shit list." This put me in a position in which I didn't want to end up. However, I had to find out who was responsible for causing my predicament. So, in the spirit of fairness, karma has her own agenda of balancing the scales of justice. The ideal time is when all of the crew is stuck on the sub, trapped and no where to go. I saw the need to take a (self-defense position) regarding the matter. My survival instincts were still intact, as we'll wait and see how the situation pans out. If Mr. Happy's wife did in fact cut him off, he well deserved it.

What I call the designated period of fun and games aboard the Grant is about to begin. This is a new concept for me, I guess I'll just join the fun. There were no actual acts of mutiny intended, just fun and games. It's a quiet understanding among the officers and the en-listed crew. Mutiny, in most cases, occurs from the bottom up. What's it called when it occurs from the top down? I'm referring to Mr. Hap-py...he got the ball rolling. Once we get underway, sea time has a way of changing people. The boat's population is a conglomerate of sailors, innocent or guilty, steadfast or audacious, those with good or insub-ordinate behavior, a basic bag of shit-stirrers. Everyone of the crew is capable of becoming a "shit stirrer." It's just human nature within our conclave of undersea, isolated "world of submarine talented mutants." Who will be capable of finding the guilty when things go awry of a crew of 140? We're all stuck surrounded in tight quarters with trouble makers hidden among us, and they will be hard to spot.

I predict there will be much giving and receiving of both good and bad idle gossip. And there's the Practical Jokesters, they can pounce at any time. However, it will be accomplished with stealth and silence, without broadcasting the results. There is are a secret cluster of waiting individuals who are ready to spring into action to send their messages. I foresee praise in some cases, and much wound licking in others before the patrol ends. (The result of vicious rumors can sometimes feel like a contact sport). It's time to even the score with those who thought they got away with it. Keep looking over your shoulder, you know who you are. Your past transgressions will sneak up to bite you in the buttocks. Besides, learn to pick a fight with someone your own size. "Status and position of ranking really doesn't matter, it's the size of your balls that count." (Section101: submarine sneak attack manual of mutant sailors). All done in good clean fun.

WAITING FOR OUR SUB ~

The Ford Island sub barracks is where I met my roommate Chris. My job was stationed in front of the building checking-in Grant sailors into our section of the barracks. Our section was located on the first floor that occupied the large, stucco, two story building. It was amazing the Japanese missed this giant target during the bombing raids on Pearl Harbor. I was seated at a table in front of the building outside on the lawn, when a physically fit and squared away sailor stepped up to offer me a hand shake. He was short in height and had good posture. I stood up to greet him. "Chris Wenzl" he said, as we shook hands using firm grips. He was not rushed, as he grabbed a chair and sat next to me to talk. He spoke clearly, and had a strong presence about him with a likable personality. Chris was also assigned to the Grant. He was working full-time at the EM Club (the enlisted men's club) across the harbor and was waiting for the Grant to return from patrol, as we all were. The EM Club was a huge and modern bar and restaurant. Located on a slight rise overlooking the other side of the harbor, it had an upscale setting for the sailors to bring their girlfriends and wives. I mentioned to Chris I'll be looking to rent an apartment in Waikiki soon and I will need a roommate to share the space. "Would you be interested? "Yes" he said with enthusiasm, as if he was honored in my asking him. "Great, we'll stay in touch and work out the details" I answered. My choice was quick in asking, but Chris was sincere, reliable, and seemed to be trustworthy. My instinct told me he was the right person as a roommate. Getting the ok from the club manager, Chris said he would borrow some items from work to supply our empty kitchen. Our food was bought from the food commissary at Hickam Airbase and the local markets near the apartment.

Once we moved into our new place and settled into a routine, I got sidetracked into a lifestyle that got me spoiled. It was a taste of freedom, living apart from the sub base, and led to my addiction of an independent style of living. It was all about home cooked meals and having friends over. It was going out and staying out late at night with no one to answer to. Absolutely no limits until you ran short of money. The cabaret clubs were open until 3 am, offering many kinds of late night socializing. It was quite a contrast to "lights out at 10 pm" at the Ford Island barracks.

I was headed for the beach one afternoon, but instead, I got suddenly side tracked. I ended up trading my six pack of Primo beer for a steak dinner with the cooks at the Reef Hotel. This occurred as a spontaneous reaction to the drifting aroma of charbroiled steaks as I walked pass the kitchen's open door. I couldn't resist not having a great steak. The smell grabbed me and pulled me back. I stuck my head in the opening and yelled; "who wants to trade an ice-cold beer for a steak dinner?" The word "beer," immediately caught the cook's attention. The duty chef and his assistant came running to the door without hesitation. Primo beer was locally produced in Hawaii, and everybody drank it, especially the locals. It was at the low end of the beer spectrum, but it was a cheap thirst quencher. Primo cost only $2.00 for a six pack of stubby glass bottles. The kitchen back door of the Reef Hotel was aways open. The back of the Reef Hotel was a public access and walk-way that led to the beach.

It was a handy opportunity for a cumshaw (a sailor's perk). I came out best of the trade, but they needed that libation to cool down. A cold beer working over a hot grill makes everyone happy. The swaps happened only a few times. I didn't want to cause any trouble for the three cooks, but the $15.00 steak dinner swap was well worth the trouble for me. The duty chef handed the charred medium steak dinner to me on a real plate, with knife and fork nestled under tinfoil. Thanks, I said, "I'll return the plate tomorrow." He thanked me twice for the Primo. It's comforting to know that my six pack of Primo Beer purchased from the ABC Store, would wind up being such a great investment.

Everything seemed to come together at the new paradise retreat. A ton of stuff showed up at our place that Chris borrowed from the EM Club, even including cloth dinner napkins. He didn't skimp on anything. He delivered the stuff using the club's work truck. I considered my time in Hawaii like a working vacation. Living off-base was an adventure, discovering new things and meeting new friends. We were accepted by our neighbors as residential locals. It was an eye-opener in choosing from all the available opportunities that came our way. Just to be around to take advantage of them like anyone else, I couldn't ask for more. During my time there, my mind wandered so far from the navy, I needed to remind myself that going to sea was just around the corner. Getting caught up with the local heartbeat of activity, I was easily swallowed by my surroundings. I was considered a local guy, by the locals and tourists. It's amazing what a brief suntan can do. It's sort of like changing into a natural chameleon disguise.

I was overrun with the abundance of opportunities that came my way, a case of being the right person, in the right place. But, the truth of a sudden departure was to be an underlying problem. Even though, being a part-time resident was a welcoming life-line to my existence, living the life as a vagabond sailor in paradise didn't mix well with the reality of being tied to my other underlying obligation, the navy. These were the risks and rewards of living two separate conflicting lives. They were driven by a impossible timetable of three months here and three months away. The odds of achieving any real headway was against me. So this time, I had to walk away from it all. Going to sea was a thorn in my side, an untimely interruption for making plans outside the navy. They were placed on hold until I returned...if still available. Leaving and dropping everything midstream didn't sit well with me. I had fears of the same nightmare reoccurring again, under this same program of "traveling back and forth." I just wanted to stay there a bit longer, to solidify a more permanent foothold before leaving. But the "rat maze" was beckoning. Ahead and waiting every three months of navy obligations with sixty-five days of that, under sea. It was a lousy and untimely reason for abandoning my Shangri-La. Duty calls, paradise beckons, and life ahead doesn't blend well for me. It appears to be another regular heaven and hell situation.

NO MORE BARRACKS ~

Returned from patrol, and the first month of R&R consisted of just phone in musters. It was a form of roll call without your actual physical presence. This made living away from the base such a great pleasure. One month was almost enough time to forget about the ravages of sea time. Following the first 30 days of R&R, the entire crew of the Grant was required to assemble at a formal muster in front of the ship's office on Ford Island. This meant reporting in full uniform.

At the muster, the crew gathered in a loose military formation, while the senior staff related any pertinent information to the crew. This included information that occurred over the past thirty days, and also facts that were given regarding the last patrol. We were informed of the status of some crew members, such as transfers to other duty stations, other subs in the fleet, school enrollments, achievement awards that were earned, advancements in rank, scuttlebutt about divorces, and the unfortunate few that had passed away…some crew members even having committed suicide.

Since that muster, my daily routine consisted of catching the ferry and reporting to the ship's office for work assignments. Quite often, we were handed off to the Master at Arms of the sub barracks. Once a week, I would stay over extra hours to stand the evening fire watch. Each submarine section of the barracks volunteered someone to stand fire watch. The one-man detail was walking around carrying a flashlight, same as a security guard. Echoes of snoring and the odor of lingering cigarettes kept me company throughout the watch. At times, an increasing number of empty racks appeared in the barracks, a signal that more sailors were moving out of the barracks as the stagnation there had grown thicker. Everyone started to get the picture. The Ford Island barracks sucks.

Life in the Ford Island barracks, surrounded by this primitive-military culture, was too dull and simplistic for me a life that offered more options for excitement was found only outside the base. Ten cent movies with five cent popcorn was the draw to the movie theatre located just around the corner of the barracks. It consisted of 1950s movie technology, just too outdated. Entertainment in the barracks was sitting on your bunk, cold showers, writing letters, or sleeping. Another fine activity was participating in the all-night poker games and eating out of the vending machines scattered about the hallway barracks. There was one pay phone in the hallway that was busy most of the time. Contraband of beer and various liquors would surface to break the boredom. Boozing it up would become standard for the evening entertainment. I didn't even have an assigned rack, but just in case, I maintained a locker for my uniform and an overnight kit, and a towel in case of an unexpected stay over. Based on the number of empty bunks and lockers to choose from, I wasn't alone in the hunt for more fun outside the base. Being here was depressing, and a total contrast with the one I led on the beach. I'm sure the the the sub barracks was headed for a complete vacancy. My thought was everyone was leaving to avoid getting marooned there. The barracks door needed a sign that read: "vacancy," blinking non-stop in bright red.

Because the Ford Island barracks were livable, yet condemned, all submarine sailors, including those on the Grant, had a choice of living here or off-base. My next hurdle was how to keep the apartment while we were at sea. Three months in, three months out at sea, was the same schedule throughout my sub career on the Grant. I was a Gold Crew member assigned to the Grant. Our crew lucked out, catching summertime and Christmas time rotation, which fell on our "off period." These were the best times of the year. The Blue Crew was our relief crew that went to sea when we were off. Living away from the base was going to be costly. Maybe the move off-base was going to create an unforeseen financial problem for me, but I'd deal with that later. Staying there in the sub barracks in order to save money didn't appeal to me. I felt sorry for those who stayed. I'd rather be happy and broke. Get me away from these doldrums. Finding a place of solitude with no one else around would be a fresh start. I wanted to reengage the world with simplicity on my own terms, with control over my own destiny. The R&R period belonged to me. I wanted to claim this time by starting with a clean slate. I needed to distance myself from the submarine mindset. That meant getting farther away from these barracks, which was a place soon to be abandoned by all.

I suspected my sanity would be stretched to its limit by the end of my first patrol. I needed to distance myself sooner than I thought. After all, how much can a person take? I couldn't stand my free time being around the crew. Sea time was punishing enough and an indicator to move somewhere more pleasant. Both my brain and sanity would need recuperation time back to normalcy, along with finding some open spaces to stretch out and relax. I had a need for more variety. Although chasing bikinis and drinking home made wine coolers were endemic to my human nature, it became my secondary choice. Getting my mental state (de-fuzzing my brain) and physical health back in order was important too. I was looking for more substance to my life. A good start would be breathing some fresh air and having sunshine on my body for a great tan. This was my recipe for feeling human again. Not seeing another sailor, nor thinking about the navy for a change would also be an improvement for a fresh start. My soul needed some time alone to thoroughly mend.

SETTLING IN ~

It was around the summer of 1967, and I had my first patrol under my belt. It was time to revisit and relearn the celebrated Waikiki Beach. There it was....three miles of pristine beach, hotels, restaurants and bars that lined the ocean's edge of this mammoth sandy crescent. Even though I lived only blocks away from there, it was like visiting an old friend every time I returned to the beach. Waikiki beach, by noon, displayed a blinding array of colorful bikinis as far as the eye could see. My other eye was lustfully scanning those sun baked beauties that my first eye had missed. Living two blocks from the ocean with proximity to everything, we didn't miss out on much. Our apartment was on Nohonani Street, Betty's place. We had many good times there. There were always visitors that dropped by our apartment. Many of them were just neighbors in the building. One day Chris and I met three ladies from Oregon. They lived at the Governor Cleghorn, a newer high rise condo located seven blocks from us. We socialized with them and hung out together. We played tennis, went to the movies, attended free concerts in the park, trips to the beach and lots of hiking. It was an affordable dutch treat dating solution.

Occasionally, a few guys from the boat dropped by for a visit. We rented Betty's place for a little over a year and were sad to leave. I scouted out the area, and just by chance, I discovered a better living situation at 471 Seaside Avenue, located just five streets over. It was another rare find and we needed to grab it soon. It was an extra large, one-bedroom bungalow cottage, almost forgotten, yet a cool, vintage, classic. Preserved as a left over from WW II, it was situated in a perfect setting. Still covered in its original faded paint and located right on the street, it gave us easy access for meeting people while sitting out front. Some evenings we'd take a walk along the Ala Wai Canal located at the end of the block.

The Islander hotel owned the cottages. This cottage was up for rent and the best of five separate units that were grouped together. It was the only one available. The rent was right, so I leased the place so we could move in immediately. Rent was a blistering two hundred a month. At that time, sub sailors received an extra $65 per month as hazardous duty pay. Later, we collected two more part-time roommates to defray the cost of rent. They were trustworthy guys off another boomer. Our schedules fell opposite of each other, so the cottage was always occupied. Our rental budget shrank to a mere fifty bucks each per month. It was a better arrangement and we seldom saw each other. I was the self appointed house master. I found the place and my name was on the lease. The cottage stayed clean and organized. Rules were followed. Life in Waikiki just got better. It was like "dying and going to paradise," and I was living proof. Getting the other two roommates was the key in keeping the cottage while we were at sea. The extra rent money gave us a little more freedom to our budget. That small amount of money didn't seem like much, but every penny counted. Remember, officer scrooge stiffed us, creating a shortfall to our paychecks.

Living life was coming together nicely after the move to the cottage. It seemed like most mornings we would check into our local coffee shop on Kalakaua Avenue, the main drag in Waikiki. We would also track our weight by stepping on the five cent scale that was available on the street for public use. It was easy to read with its large round thirty inch dial. We ate healthy. Mostly we had chef salads that I prepared to keep us in shape. We consumed homemade wine coolers before heading out for the evening. Living within walking distance of reaching everything we wanted to do, Waikiki was the center of activity where something was happening around the clock, day or night. Truly, "The Life of Riley."

My roommate Chris and I spent time that was easy on the pocketbook. There was a money crunch between the two of us, the greenbacks were becoming scarce. This was the sacrifice we made living away from the barracks, a sacrifice to free housing and meals. Our independence came at a steep price. Cheap entertainment was always on our minds. When we were short on money, we had to get creative about dating. One time on a date, to keep my spending in check, we toured the harbor where all the luxury boats were docked. We enjoyed visiting with the boat people who resided there. During the outing we indulged in a cocktail, a cup of coffee and a beach hotel dessert. Susan, my date, said it was the best time she ever experienced. Some days later, Chris met the manager of the apartments across the street from the cottage. He gave him permission to use their swimming pool, since we were neighbors living across the street. Chris used the pool for his morning swims. He jumped over the short fence located next to the sidewalk to enter the pool.

Everything went well, until one day, Chris was rejected because of an unannounced management change. He discovered his swimming rights were terminated, and Chris was upset about it, but soon got over it. One day, I walked by the swimming pool which was located along side the sidewalk, and I noticed the color of the pool was a bright yellow-green neon color. The water appeared to be glowing and could be interpreted as radioactive. Concern from the office staff was apparent, no one who lived there swam in the pool for days. It brightened up during the night when the pool lights were turned on. I concluded a navy dye-marker was used to brightened up the water. Dye markers are used in coloring sea water for rescues. It's a concentrated substance, so just imagine what it did to the swimming pool water. The mysterious incident made me wonder how that happened? The management said that a sailor who just moved in upstairs, threw something in the pool the other evening. The incident was apparently witnessed by another renter that lived there. I really didn't care. I soon forgot about the colorful prank. Regardless, I thought the newly colored water was an improvement. There was no harm done. No residual foul odor was noticed and the color dissipated over time. The incident was soon forgotten. Chris shrugged his shoulders and didn't mention anything about it.

BROKE IN PARADISE ~

Remember, the first month coming off patrol and returning to Hawaii was marked by "phone-in musters only." A simple phone call before 8am was the accepted method for checking in. This was the standard policy for the sailors who lived off-base, and was the navy's version of keeping tabs on us. That way, they knew you were still on the island and hadn't abandoned them. Free as a bird, but short on change was my predicament. Coming off patrol, everyone on our boat was flush with cash and paychecks, except for the hard-core poker losers. There's something about living in a tourist mecca that is like a blackhole on cash. One day, you reach in your pocket and you find zilch. Even your pocket change has vanished. The last place you want to be stuck with empty pockets is here in paradise. My reserve funds were held back for rent and other emergencies. So, in order to cure the zilch-dilemma, finding a short-part-time job became paramount. During my time in Waikiki, a few part-time jobs became available that I worked to make my financial ends meet. Painting the upstairs gift shop at the International Market Place was a welcoming pay check. Flipping burgers was another. Another job was working security at the Dole Pineapple plant. Chris's job was as assistant executive chef at the enlisted men's club (largest in the world at the time). His earnings were a big help in healing our financial situation; although, his boss, the chef, was gay and wanted to bed his young ass. He refused and eventually quit his job.

I met Maggie during my daily walk back to the cottage. Using a short-cut through the maze of gift shops, bars, and restaurants, allowed me to pass by her shop through to the other end of the maze. I would stop and chat with her to keep up with the happenings. She was quiet, but always friendly to me. She worked in a shop called "Mary Jane's," located in the back of the "International Market Place." It was a hippy shop. Another merchant of the psychedelic fad that invaded the music and dress culture which dominated Waikiki culture during this time period. Even my roommate Chris wore a big colored hat and walked around strumming his guitar. He had a cigarette hanging from his mouth to fit the part perfectly.

Waikiki embraced the Hippy Era during the 1960's. There were a lot of tie dyed folks living in this part of town (near the "Jungle," long since gone). I remember "Sergeant Peppers Lonely Hearts Club Band," Beatles album was out. (I heard today's pristine condition of that album is worth $25,000) The "Power House Saloon" was a beer bar located behind Maggie's shop. The place was packed with patrons after 10am that featured loud jukebox music and endless Primo Beer flowing from the kegs. Primo Beer was produced locally and "The Power House" was their biggest beer consuming account in the State of Hawaii. I heard the saloon poured up to 60-90 kegs of Primo daily, which represented hundreds of pitchers of beer. This puts a new twist on the standard concept of just another "watering hole." Patrons also consumed several fifty pound burlap bags of free peanuts in the shell. Beer was $1.25 a glass, not enough to keep me out. It came as the price of dinner in a shell, all you can eat, and all you can drop on the floor. Another spot where I could be found was my favorite coffee shop, the "Outrigger Restaurant." The restaurant was near the cottage and I worked the grill part-time. Occasionally, but only when I was needed to fill-in. "The Attic," a popular upstairs cocktail lounge, served double shot cocktails with pupus (bowls of appetizers) for ninety cents. It was the local's hangout and I stopped in there too. During this time, the movie makers were in town filming "Tora, Tora, Tora," and later "The Hawaiians." They hired stand-ins (extras) for the movies. There was also a casting call for "Hawaii Five O." There seemed to be a lot of work available, and I missed out on many of these opportunities. The filming schedule was out of sync with the submarine schedule, and just think, I could have been an extra and appeared on Hawaii-Five-O. This is a great place to juice it up with a small acting role and possible romance. Romance is another extra, why not have fun with it?

Once again, my pressing agenda was focused on preparing for sea. I was certainly not looking forward to encountering the second half of sub quals. Returning to sea was an irritant in a sudden leaving of my comfy life. The dilemma was breaking off any connections that I had established with my local friends. In many cases, I left without any explanation to those who needed one. Returning to the confines of "rats in a can" didn't offer any sort of closer-bonding with the navy. This raised the quandary of adjusting to the "in port and out at sea dilemma." It seemed like it was getting the best of me. It was another grin and bear it moment, which I had to magically adapt to, and mentally retreat from, the good life. Then deal with another round of annoying submarine hell. I found that preparing for sea was worse that actually being there.

AN UNEXPECTED SURPRISE ~

During the remainder of my time in Waikiki, I had no choice but to set all money dating aside. Dating, and having a good time were just too expensive. In some cases, just meeting someone for a date, would indirectly cost me money. My desire for dating was always there, but my financial deficit held me back. I was still barely financially afloat. But, I wasn't destitute enough to move back to the barracks. Much of my spare time was sitting on the beach, hiking about, or visiting friends. How my time was spent was important. Freedom away from the base, and being immersed in rest and relaxation certainly made it worthwhile. This "is" paradise. Receiving the extra $65 per month in hazardous duty pay did matter in having a great time. Sometimes, to make better use of my time, the ladies from the mainland provided lunch or dinner as an exchange for me being their tour guide for the day.

One day, Maggie caught my attention. I stopped by her shop many times to visit and make small talk. Apparently over time, we became close friends, much closer than I expected. This time it was different. I was seeing those extra smiles on her face. She was being more open and friendlier than usual. She started to show interest in me and I sensed she was reaching out from her longtime loneliness. Having observed her actions in the past, I'd noticed that she had turned down guys while being approached by them at the shop. I didn't know what to expect when her focus turned to me. But things seemed to have changed. Maggie reached out to make the first move.

The cottage was a short distance from her place of work. I'd invited her over to the cottage many times, but in the past she was a no-show. One afternoon, she unexpectedly showed up at the door. It was her first time there and our first time being together alone in privacy. She seemed relaxed and I sensed fooling around was on her mind. I read it in her eyes, sort of a dead give away. Our chemistry easily bonded together, as if we were two lost souls finding each other after a long dry spell of solitude. It caught us both by surprise. We were drawn together like heated magnets laced with super glue, embracing a tender round of "letting nature take its course." We were inseparable, traveling from one room to the next, stripping down beyond our tan lines along the way. Finally, after a lengthy round of heavy breathing, we ended up in the kitchen for a glass of water to cool down. I must confess, the older 1950's vintage kitchen table was most accommodating.

I moved our water glasses away from the danger zone. Leaning over, I drew the curtains shut. Our eyes were transfixed on the table top. With a faint smile, we climbed aboard for a first time adventure. Thoroughly lost in our excitement, we must have covered the entire surface, skidding across every square inch of the table top, stopping only once in fear of falling off. We laid there laughing with exhaustion, hearing the chirping noise of the friction. What a way to finish an afternoon. It was just what we needed to break the ice with each other. It was better than talking about the weather and finishing with a drink on the front porch. I didn't realize Maggie was so adventurous. Neither did she. It was a fortunate moment that brought out the best in the both of us. It was just one of those rare occasions. But, I am sad to say, it never happened again.

The afternoon was just a one time fling of uncontrolled self-indulgence for each of us. We'd shared a spontaneous moment that neither one of us could pass up. Later, she returned to her former shyness, and to that reserved person that I once knew. Looking back, she wasn't as innocent as I thought. Someone once said, "never pass judgement on quiet people." That I believe, and have found to be true. This is a story that I someday can pass along. It belongs in the wisdom and answer column of my mind.

From that time forward, I would smile, looking at that flimsy formica kitchen table, thanking it in silence for not collapsing beneath us. I was glad that it held together by the sudden attack of wear and tear. It was still a keeper. More rickety than ever, but with a new history.

WHO ARE WE? ~

The U.S. Naval Submarine Fleet, is best known as "The Silent Service." Even today, submarines still remain shrouded in mystery. Their functions, operations, and other unknown aspects of their existence are kept secret. Submariners give life and purpose to their existence, faced with the complexities of underwater life, while trapped in confined conditions. We operate beneath the surface, surrounded in peril of the possibility of equipment failure, pummeled by sea pressures, and tracked by an known enemy makes it that way. It makes no difference, we're on patrol to fulfill our appointed mission and destiny. As trusted individuals, bound together in this life and death setting, and having volunteered for submarine duty, we are committed for the long run. There is little room for error in this unique world in which we live. We are watchful and vigilant for any shipboard emergencies, any one of which can spell disaster for us by charging the ultimate price. Or we may survive each patrol, a bit older and wiser.

Integrity among us is our strength and it's crucial that we believe in this reality. The submarine crew retains the right in choosing who will make the cut, mentally and physically. Those who aren't worthy in passing our judgement and scrutiny, will fail in becoming one of us. We are strenuously tested to qualify as competent crew members, all meeting the same rigorous standards for submarine qualifications. We are held in trust to perform our duties while being underpaid and probably under appreciated. Nevertheless, we are here to save the world. And being the last bastion of sanity in preventing or allowing nuclear conflict, we are the silent heroes you never hear about.

The mission is the big picture. As guardians of the peace, we are here to preserve it. We operate undetected with stealth and silence as we set out to patrol. Our enemy silently and secretly attempts to trace our footprint in the ocean. It's a continuous game of cat and mouse. Our sixteen nuclear missiles are ready to release their fury at a moment's notice. There are forty-one Boomers just like us, all hidden beneath the oceans and seas spread across the world, waiting patiently. We are the last deterrent in the face of our enemy that poses a threat against the United States and our allies. We are poised to spring into action, to do the unthinkable if provoked. Until such time, life onboard continues to be status quo. As long as the Captain doesn't get too incensed, everything remains cool. For the crew of the U.S.S. Ulysses S. Grant, this is our home away from home. This is who we are.

CHANGING ENVIRONMENTS ~

Living within the confined spaces of a submarine requires mental flexibility, and the ability to adapt to the fluctuating realities within these ever changing human parameters. A different focus and outlook in preparation by the crew is a "heads up" in dealing with these situations. The human psyche can be transformed through many unsettling changes; then can change the mental and physical pressures of the patrol. This could be interpreted as psychological manifestations that can spread among crew members. It can't be avoided. We all must focus our energy and deal with it individually, creating and following your own rules where sometimes there are none. No one manages our minds. It takes a nebulous form and you can't put your finger on it. However, the unaware, such as the non-qual, (anyone, not qualified in submarines) will be unexpectedly ambushed and toyed-with throughout the patrol. And his naive inexperience will enter several surrealistic encounters. It's a sharp learning curve, and will come in rapid succession with no rest.

This will become an intrusive way of life for the non-qual. He will need to feel out the differences of truth and creative bullshit. It all comes down to training and who can you trust. The non-qual gets blindsided by this activity and will be scratching his head thinking "What the fuck happened?" Dealing with his dilemma, he needs to reorganize and sharpen his wits by ignoring the negative aspects. He needs to stay on point learning his assigned job, and to stay focused on qualifying, and definitely to stay off the delinquent list by studying each system on a schedule. He needs to function while being sleep deprived and mentally spent, all while retaining the information he just learned, and brushing off endless badgering.

All non-quals encounter teasing, bullying and other unchartered forms of testing or hazing by the crew. Unforeseen mental confusion may collide with his normal thinking patterns. A little added stress, (as an indulgence of the crew) can be applied in elevating the situation to cull the unreliable. Once the non-qual is qualified in submarines, all absurd treatment will disappear. His status will change to that of a trusted and respected member of the crew. He now knows most of what keeps the heart of the steel beast pulsating.

For the non-qual, it seems impossible to see an end to the long, drawn out process. It's a double whammy for him. He has the pleasure of repeating this "nightmare scenario" by returning the following patrol to finish up his submarine qualifications. The non-qual, returning from a three month break in Hawaii, needs to pick up the pace to get back where he left off, and will reluctantly continue living this ridiculous process. Hopefully, drinking himself into oblivion while on his R&R didn't wash away many of those memorized facts and systems that he needed to retain for the upcoming patrol. It was time to take an in depth look, reviewing that lost information and getting back into the rhythm of the patrol.

Chris was able to qualify in submarines in one patrol and also made 3rd class Sonar Tech on his second patrol. One smart guy, and being one hell of a roommate.

PSYCHOLOGICAL GAME PLAYING ~

It's part of the crew's ritual screwing with your mind. Sort of nudging you over the edge into unfamiliar territory. It's all part of "the game." Sometimes the game produces real and negative consequences with very serious and damaging effects. Psychological "gaming" can be light-hearted; or serious warfare among the crew members, at many different levels, depending on approach and attitude at the time, and an ongoing process.

You can be the one who messes with someone else, or you can be a recipient of such callousness. Or, you can be an observer seeking neutrality. After the patrol ends, devastating results can unfortunately be counted. At the end of our patrol, it was rumored there were nine divorces that occurred, and only one crew member checking in with the "professionals" for a head adjustment. There was a newlywed who thought his wife left him and spent all his money, and a ship's doctor hooked on heroin, who later died. Another rumor pointed to a successful suicide, after the wife and children left the sailor while out on patrol. These are just a few unfortunate events that may or may not have occurred. Some are based on unsubstantiated rumors, the others are documented facts.

This is the dark side of submarine duty. Nothing learned from our patrol can be trusted as truth. These events seemed so mythical at the time, happening in silence and secrecy. It's a shocking eye opener of what possibly occurred during our patrols. A "healthy outlook" is for everyone to remain normal after the patrol. I thought I was the only one who discovered the dark side of this sub culture. Every man must find various methods to cope: music, sleep, food, movies, books, further schooling and classes, just to name a few distractions. Oh yeah, and lots of one handed love affairs.

These actions match the makeup of a crew at these particular durations of time, the results of the "end game" after returning from sea. Some have provocative results. Some give or some receive, but there is no escape, especially for the "rats in a can." And which end of the stress spectrum you will fall to can happen without control if you're not very careful. Subconsciously you can slip into a realm wherein your actions can be defined by the crew. And neutrality is very tough in a world of self preservation. Bending reality to accommodate your perspective is one way of handling it. The mind will either take sides, or recede into itself. Were these sad events truth or fiction? The answers of why?, unfortunately, lie with the injured or dead.

A QUICK TOUR ~

Living in a confined space such as this three dimensional "rat maze" existence, requires physical changes to blend with the environmental variations. Walking, reaching, stretching, and other normal movements need restraints and adjustments in preventing bumps, bruises, slips, and falls. You are hazardous to your own health. Until adjustments are made to your physical surroundings, you need to slow down. Safety first! Changes are needed in small spaces, within an even smaller world.

There are also a wide range of emotional changes everyone is confronted with. Making adjustments in self-control is tweaked each patrol. We don't talk about it. We keep to ourselves. We self-manage our thoughts in very silent privacy. We are our own sounding board, we monitor ourselves as needed. Occasionally in the morning, I'd surrender to my psychological inner-self by talking to that trusted familiar face in the mirror while shaving. There are other notable changes, such as your eyes, adjusting for short and for distance focusing. One reason for this, there is no long distant viewing down here. The farthest you can see is a little over 30-40 feet. So you strain your eyes to test for distance when focusing on something or someone.

And there is a slight chill in the air in order to keep the computers and other heat sensitive equipment from malfunctioning. The AC works well down here. It's always cooling everything down, including us. The AC is a life saver compared to the burning heat and humidity of the Guamanian humid hell. Throughout the boat, there is a faint odor of diesel fuel. And there's no escaping it. It's part of the permanent-makeup of the submarine. It's said that there's a thin film of oil everywhere on subs, including the coffee. All the aspects of what I imagine or life of a cave dweller to be.

The majority of the compartments are occupied with the engine room, power station, weaponry, various sized tanks, lots of machinery, and other ancillary environmental control machines. Compartments are connected end to end with water tight doors for flood control measures. Ladders, short hallways, and some staircases are narrow and tight. These separate and connect the different levels, changing the spaces, pathways, and configurations of those compartments.

The remaining space is for the crew, but there is not much remaining. If it wasn't for the popularity of the crew aways sleeping (up to one third of the boat's population 24/7), the boat's open spaces would be hard pressed to accommodate the crew as a whole. The major open areas which allow the crew to gather are in the lower two levels of the operations compartment. Common areas to gather for the crew are in the mess deck during meal time. (Officers are excluded. They have their own space separate from ours). There is a small room designated as the library. It is no more than a small room with three chairs and a counter offering of some outdated paperback books. As you can see, there is a limited space. "Frenchy" (John Lemieux) often played his guitar in the library.

Limitations concerning privacy rest on a knife's edge of nonexistence. An offering for privacy would be sitting on the crapper to cogitate your daily constitution. "Behind the locked door" duplicates as a sensory deprivation chamber. Amazingly, privacy can be created within the smaller world of a stainless steel stall within the small world of a submarine within the deep dark abyss on our beautiful blue marble, lost in the vastness of an inner space.

Outside of the library is a gaming table with L shaped built-in seating against the wall with a few additional chairs. Another table with seats is situated across the lounge area. This small and trivial space is our "crews lounge." It doesn't make sense. The smallest area is host to the largest part of the crew (with the exception of the mess deck). No wonder we're fighting for elbow room.

This is an activity center where noisy, nightly games such as poker, bridge, and cribbage are held. The poker games are money games. Betting with real money adds to the excitement. It's good spirited fun, which is needed. But it can get out of hand. It's risking your entire sea pay at the table, win or lose. Gambling can be a very serious activity. And it's a big risk for the married guys. You can hear the rowdiness from the players and the spectators gathered around the gaming table. A total crowd of 10 counting players, who know they need to shut the fuck up. Losing at the table can be paramount to divorce-making in progress. Sometimes the Captain would put a $500 cap on poker losses for each person for that patrol.

Berthing is near the crews lounge. Migrating noises from everywhere filter in to disrupt sleeping. Poker games continue around the clock, except for leaving to stand watch, or get a meal or drills. Is it gambling fever or just plain boredom that drives some excitement into our mundane lives, with the exception of pop-up drills.

Drills are irritating and can appear any time, day or night. Night drills deprive sleepers from sleep; and during the day, it's a unscheduled wake-up call. The nickel coke machine is located down near the lounge. Coke is served in small waxed cups that drop down before getting filled (sometimes). I have never witnessed open containers of booze, but I know those cups were laced later with liquor. Many times I worked the TDU (trash disposal unit) room crushing empty booze bottles, glass popping, a dead giveaway.

Bourbon, brandy, and rum mix best with coke. Down in crew's berthing area, closet drinkers can hide their habit very well. I met some crew mates who were self confessed alcoholics. They choose FBM duty over other submarine duty. It offers a longer time at sea. And thus a longer time away from the bottle. Perhaps a better chance to dry out, or maybe the opposite.

Cigarette smoking is allowed everywhere except in some working areas. Sleeping quarters, and in the mess hall during meals, are also off limits. Occasional fires would pop up in the TDU room. A hot cigarette ash carelessly left, might end up in the garbage and start a blaze.

How do we address so much cigarette smoke in the air? One of my collateral duties was taking readings of the atmospheric gases throughout the boat to maintain clean breathable air. This is accomplished by monitoring readings in 30 minute intervals using the atmosphere analyzer located in the Control Room. A sniffer within the unit can detect levels of gases throughout the boat in each compartment. The function of the analyzer is to detect parts per million (ppm) levels of hazardous gases in the atmosphere. Most are from cigarette smoke (carbon monoxide). Six or more other gases are noted in a ledger to track their concentrations. If the ppm levels of the hazardous gases exceed the acceptable range of breathable atmosphere, the air is cleaned (using the CO-H2 burners and CO2 scrubbers).

The air is sucked up using vacuum fans in the ventilation system (a network of interconnecting ventilation piping connecting all compartments with their related equipment). The contaminated air is sent to and through the burners and scrubbers located in the machinery spaces. The contaminants are burned using intense heat or chemically scrubbed with lithium bromide. The air is then cooled purified and returned into the atmosphere. Residual contaminants are neutralized with chemicals then discharged to sea during the process. The air is continuously recycled using this method until the air is completely clean. Pure oxygen is bled into the boat's atmosphere to maintain at least 20%. Breathable air within a submarine is cleaner by comparison than the outside atmosphere.

In the case of a reported fire onboard the submarine, and if the sub is filling with toxic-choking smoke, the boat simultaneously rises to a snorkel depth and raises the snorkel mast. (the subs' exhaust pipe) The snorkel mast and Diesel engine are used for emergency smoke evacuation during a fire. Once the fire is extinguished, fresh air is recycled throughout the boat. It's sort-of-like everyone rolling down the windows when somebody farts in the car. Everybody can relate to that.

The galley and the dining area are located in midlevel ops. It is busiest and noisiest during feeding time. Food is a homing beacon for the crew to gather in one place to chow down. The galley cranks out four meals a day for a hungry crew of 140 and coincides with four hour shifts a day. Breakfast, lunch, dinner, and mid-rats are the four meals served daily, with leftovers to be snacked on all day 'til gone. Weight gain is a problem for everyone, with the exception of the few skinny ones blessed with skinny genes. Believe it or not, some sailors stay in the navy because of all the food they can eat. They're most likely from the poorer parts of the country, and that food was scarce during their upbringing. Think about coming to an all you can eat meal four times a day. That would be hard to turn down. I also met a sailor who was issued his first pair of shoes when he joined the navy.

The dining area (crew's mess) has eight tables with bench seating, six to a table. There are three feeding sessions each meal, stragglers dropping by later. The boat's galley is relatively small, but operates efficiently. Maybe three workers can fit into this fast moving 24/7 hub of activity. Non essential personnel are ordered to keep out. Aside from the on duty cook there is always at least one mess-cook who assists him, usually a non-qual. After cleaning up the mess hall, scrubbing pots, pans and running plates through the dishwasher, the non-qual assists with food prepping for the next meal. He retrieves the food from their storage spaces hidden throughout the boat. It's not a simple matter. Much time is spent retrieving the next meals from all of the several storage areas. Some storage spaces are both hidden and located far from the galley.

Navigating through the boat locating food is a daily quest that includes finding and retrieving thirty-five pound bulk tins of foods hidden under the deck plates in three, long, deep, linear and different locations. The mess-cook sets up the dining room before service, and delivers platters and bowls of food during the feeding sessions. After feeding, he clears and cleans the dining room tables. His co-ordinated efforts are timed with and in-between feeding times.

The mess-cook is run ragged all day and into the night. Sometimes there are two mess-cooks assigned during the day. Late in the day the mess-cook gets to shoot trash. Sometimes there are thirty cans waiting for him. (The cans are just square flat sheets of galvanized metal that are rolled, and shaped into 12" diameter cylinders. The cans are held together with metal tabs, then the trash is inserted into them including the garbage weights and an end caps are attached). The mess cook is stuck in the TDU room for at least an hour shooting trash. The job of mess cook is the most time consuming job onboard the boat moving at a vicious non-stop pace. The mess cook begins his day by peeling one hundred pounds of potatoes using a pairing knife. Then, after waiting on the crew during chow, ends his day by sweeping and swabbing out the galley and mess-deck floors.

Sometimes he is asked to be in two places at once. The job is an all day busy mission. His job is the most important by cranking out meals to meet the demands of the assigned duty cook(s). At the days end, the mess-cook still needs to work on his submarine qualifications. Food is the only pleasurable morale factor on the boat (besides the evening movies). It is the single item in high demand by everyone on the boat. There are no acceptable screw ups or delays by the galley team's efforts.

The mess-cook is at the bottom of the totem pole and the least respected by most of the crew. The only advantage of mess cooking, is he's not stuck in one spot while working. He also receives praise when he refills the empty platters of food during the feeding sessions. He gets plenty of exercise being immersed in his arduous work. A full featured movie is shown in the dining area after evening meals. Mid rats (rations) is served not long after the movie begins. Mid rats consists mostly of sandwiches, left overs, and desserts can be picked up outside the galley on a service counter. Drink dispensers are also located there. I was one of the designated movie projectionist in the evenings, unless I was working my other job in the Control Room.

THE GALLEY LAYOUT ~

The Grant's galley is located mid-level operations compartment. The galley is sandwiched beneath the control room above and the crews lounge / berthing area below. The forward end of the galley, port side, is where the huge walk-in refrigerator is located. The walk-in freezer is across from it, 30" away. The TDU room is located in the same general area.

Despite the small size of the commercial galley, it is superbly efficient. It's a credit to the hustle of the cooking staff, and production of consistently good food and serving it on time that makes it that way. Very few complaints are heard from the staff and crew. Using only one duty cook and two mess cook per shift, the galley cranks out copious amounts of quality food (and all you can eat) to feed the large crew.

The galley serves four planned meals a day, plus daily fresh baked breads, cinnamon rolls plus assorted desserts. Snacks and leftovers are always available to the crew. Trays of these items are laid out at the pass-through area between meals. Both walk-ins are big and filled with provisions stacked up to the outward opening doors and insides, up to the ceilings. This is evidence there will never be a food shortage aboard our submarines. It's always to be prepared if our patrol is unexpectedly extended.

Having copious amounts of food on hand is a very serious issue. Just inside the door (the door opening outward) there is a wall of cases of food indicating the freezer is filled to capacity. The menu is planned so that we eat our way into the freezer. This eliminates searching for the next meal to prepare. Even our Captain gets involved with the menu planning, making sure we get the best quality of everything that's available from the sub-tender "Proteus." The Proteus is the last opportunity to top off our stores and stock up on spare parts, mostly new tools for the boat before leaving on patrol.

The freezer needs defrosting twice during the patrol. The defrosting is planned, and occurs just before the start of the evening movie. The crew, expecting the start of the movie, instead are hijacked in helping to empty the freezer in preparation for defrosting. The plan is to ensure that there is an ample number of bodies to help with the defrosting work. Hundreds of frozen cases of food are removed from the freezer and are temporarily stacked on the floor, aft of the dining area. Stacking cases on the dining tables is also utilized. The cooks co-ordinated their placements. A single line of manpower is formed to move the cases, one by one, from inside the freezer. The Congo line continues through the galley, and across the mess hall floor to be stacked just aft of the movie projector. The ice formed inside the freezer is hosed out and completely hand dried using squeegees and shammies. Now, the process is reversed for reloading the freezer. There is a one-hour delay in the showing of the movie, but well tolerated by the crew. Located on the mess deck entry wall just outside the galley is the 24/7 coffee maker and service area, 3 juice machines, and a serve-soft ice cream machine. Ice cream cones are available to anyone who wanted one. You could make them as big as you wanted.

Joe Key worked back aft in the machinery space. He said he lost his right eye two years ago when he was looking into a blocked pipe to see if it was clear. Someone turned on high pressure air to blow out the blockage. His common sense must have momentarily left him and it cost him his right eye. Regardless, he still retained his sense of humor. Since losing his eye, the navy replaced his eye with a prosthetic one. It appeared very real. I talked to Joe several times and, by looking at his face, there was no indication of a fake eye. Although, as it was made of plastic and muscles were not attached, it didn't track with his other one.

One afternoon, he was in the ice cream line to make a cone for himself. Our boat had a soft serve ice cream machine; and the only flavor was vanilla. I happened to be standing behind him, waiting my turn. He spun around and said, " Here, I made this one for you" and handed me a freshly made ice cream cone. I thanked him and went to take a bite, with his EYEBALL staring up at me. Then he said, "Oh there it is. I was looking for that" and picked off the prosthetic eyeball and licked it, then popped it back into the socket. He looked at me staring, "Are both my eyes lined up?" I replied, "Move it a little to the left...perfect." Well, it was perfectly aligned for him to look goofy and half cross-eyed. Touché. It was just a great look for this jokester. Having returned my version for a laugh, I gave him back his ice cream cone and said, "You eat it." I wonder what went through his mind the next time he looked in a mirror?

Before his shift ended, the duty cook, without fail, must break out the next days frozen cases of food for defrosting. Imagine what would happen if he forgot. Basically, all hell would break loose. So, these cardboard boxes of food are set out on the galley counters for thawing the night before. The duty cook who forgets to set them out is in deep doo-doo. From the Captain on down, through to the last man of the crew. He'll take a relentless tongue lashing.

Have you ever eaten frozen food as it is being defrosted and being cooked at the same time? It's unpalatable. I've witnessed this. For the most part, frozen or defrosting meats cooked, end up tough as shoe leather. (No microwave oven is available in our galley to expedite the defrosting time) Besides, the crew can easily detect "railroaded" chow. There is no disguising or improving the taste and texture. Perchance ketchup poured over, as a chef's enhancement.

We have a Yeoman-secretary and his job is dealing with transfers on and off the boat. He gets an earful to ship this new belly robber off the boat. This was our replacement cook with an unbelievable rank of chief cook? Despite his rank, his cooking abilities were for surface sailors (destroyers). How did he get anywhere near being promoted to chief cook, then slip through the cracks and end up on our boat? The crew was relentless in giving him verbal threats and colorful names (also behind his back) There was no where for him to hide and no forgiveness for screwing with the crew's morale by ruining the meals. He didn't surrender to the verbal insults from the crew. Mentally he was too bullheaded and stupid. And, there was no improvement in the quality of his food preparing talent. Well, I was the unexpected catalyst that assisted in changing his mind. I quietly volunteered myself as sacrificial lamb to help out regarding this problem. But, I did this at a later time, when the timing seemed right.

The crew is approximately one hundred-forty crewmen. You're probably wondering where they are found on the boat. And it's quite amazing how they all blend into the spaces of this submersible until they suddenly appear in the chow line. Not all 140 show up at once, but are scattered among the four feeding sessions. Eating is the only pleasure; and they can't afford to miss out on something good. The crew looks forward to eating simply because in most case there is nothing else to look forward to. Eating makes everyone feel better.

Visiting the chow hall daily is the morale booster all sailors need. Sitting down to a good meal is paramount in the life of a sub sailor, and offers a chance to quickly socialize with other crew members at the dining table. But, they need to eat and move on. There are four seatings to feed the entire crew. The dining room (mess hall) is the largest gathering area on the sub. The dining tables are arranged four deep with bench seating. There are two sets, port and starboard arrangements in the dining room. They are situated across from each other with an aisle between for serving. Each table accommodates six people. (Officers have their own private dining area).

The aft end of the dining tables is an open area used for a pop-up movie theatre. Against the far wall is the movie projector location. The open area is set up with folding chairs so nighty movies can be shown there. Hundreds of film canisters are stored in the missile compartment. There are many movies from which to choose. Movies are rotated or traded between other FBMs located at Guam. Food is available from the galley during the movies, including popcorn.

Hidden in the movie area ceiling is a drop-down operating table that can be utilized for any medical emergency. Like all boomers, we had a certified MD onboard the Grant. His assistant, (we named "Doc") carried a large horse needle. He flashed it at us when he was dispensing inoculations. Attached at the business end was a 6" long corkscrew shaped large diameter needle. He made it curly shaped to grab everyone's attention. So after seeing this, a regular needle didn't seem too threatening when we received our shots.

Storage on a sub is utilized where ever it can be found. The garbage weights are two pound steel rounds that come in a forty-pound box. Hundreds of the boxes are stored on the port side in the torpedo room, along with many sacks of fresh onions located up-high in a separate space. The added weight in the different sections of the boat are calculated for trimming the boat. Every nook and cranny on the sub is used for storage of food stuffs and spare parts of every kind.

The bench seats located in the dining area are a perfect example. They make for handy storage of small canned goods such as, tuna, sardines, spam, smoked oysters, etc. (One day, I even found canned lobster meat. I never saw it on any menu). Between the two rows of tables is an aisle for the mess cooks to set, serve, and clear the dining tables. There is also a pass through window to the galley, where the mess cooks pick up the platters and bowls of food during meals. It also doubles as a drop-off zone for plates and their eating utensils when the crew is finished eating.

Next to that is the open entryway into the galley. The platters and plates are made of an unbreakable plastic, composite material. If someone dropped it on the floor or threw it at you, there would be little noise. Also, some dishes go flying during "angles and dangles" (extreme maneuvers of the sub) but the "plate" would survive the impact.

Fresh fruit, vegetables, eggs and other perishables were loaded from the sub tender to us, by us, in Guam. Our freezer items, mainly meats were hand picked by "Frenchy" from the sub tender inventory. Our freezer is filled with the best meats and other frozen entrees. Steak night was selected more often in the food rotation due to its popularity, followed by lobster. The cooks bake their own bread and an entire line of baked products. During my five patrols on the Grant, we were fortunate in having the best cooks in the fleet, (except for one sub-par cook who ended up getting booted off the Grant).

John Lemieux was by far the best cook. A very popular friend to all on board. He was just a shift-cook assigned to the Grant. I enjoyed working along side him for several patrols. "Frenchy" was voted number one in our fleet, including the many surface ships. There were over sixty-ships included in the cooking competition. He won the Navy's prestigious "Ney Award," for achieving five star quality and excellence. As first prize, he was sent to the Culinary Institute of America (CIA) in Hyde Park, New York City. He was absent for one patrol on the Grant while being trained at CIA. His cooking talent was sorely missed by the crew because of an inadequate replacement cook who was eventually transferred off the boat (previously mentioned). John returned to the Grant the following patrol with two cases of Marsala wine for cooking. He was now ready for cooking some serious gourmet meals! The crew had missed his cooking and was glad upon his return. I would be remiss in not mentioning that he also attended a cooking class at the prestigious "Playboy Club" located in Italy, during the same period.

THE ART OF DINING ~

I remember sitting at the crew's dining table. I was lucky to find a spot as I'd just gotten off watch and snuck in line. The rush was on and the mess hall filled up quickly. It happen to be steak night, so I lucked out again.

As soon as we sat down, the mess cooks delivered the platters of steaks to the tables. There were six steaks to a platter, one for each of us. I saw forks lunging in front of my face, heading for the New York steaks. Mine was last on the platter. "Hurry," they yelled to me. Our empty platter, was slid to the mess cook to be refilled on his way back to the galley. "Fill it up again," they said with their mouths full and chewing up the last of their steak. The steaks were instantly scarfed up. The room became silent, only chewing was heard, as I witnessed the epitome of gluttony. Table manners didn't exist. Looking up, all the tables were scarfing down the grinds (food). It was an "all-out feeding frenzy" of sailors not sharks. When the second round of steaks hit the table, same thing happened. Men were standing up, reaching, elbowing for position, taking aim and stabbing the meat with their forks. It resembled "the last supper," submarine style. The baked spuds, veggies and breads were ignored and getting cold. Some ate the whole steak, fat, gristle, and all. The steaks disappeared so fast, I thought they were putting them in their pockets. Then the empty platter was sent back; I lost count how many times. The average sailor inhaled up to six of these perfectly grilled six-ounce steaks. However, the big eaters, "the two hundred pounders-plus" who worked back aft in the hot machinery spaces of the engine room did the most damage. They were the dominant, heavy duty chowhounds on the boat. The food didn't stand a chance with them. When they sat down to eat, they didn't slow down. For the most part, inhaling copious amounts of food on a submarine was not a case of having "eyes bigger that your stomach," it was the other way around. Some beat their own records by consuming eight lobster tails each during Sunday night dinners. Other nights offered "non-bingeing foods" such as pot roast, pork chops, meatloaf, and chicken. There was a noticeable slow down in speed eating, but they still consumed mass amounts of food. It all gave a chance for the "Food Scarfers" to ease off their eating in mass volumes and to give the toilets a break.

The chow line always formed thirty minutes before serving. The single-file line began outside of MCC (Missile Control Center) hallway. When the food was ready, everybody, one by one, scampered up the ladder, one level up, to enter the dining area. Once the dining seats were full, the food started issuing from the galley. Eating and movies were the only constant satisfaction for the crew. Just guessing, some of these guys, easily ate their weight in food during a patrol. It's a case of the old cliché, "they came aboard as sailors, and left the sub as cargo." Servings of fresh fruit for breakfast and vegetables at lunch and dinner, were an important part of daily meals. Vegetables were served in the form of mixed green salad with a choice of dressing. The crew was served the perishable greens before they turned bad, or until they were totally consumed.

In the past, lemons and oranges were used for scurvy prevention. Today, green salads and assorted fresh vegetables are served during every dinner, until we run out. These are the necessary foods for scurvy prevention. We were served every last bit of this precious food even when it turned bad. As an example, the last cases of our heads of iceberg lettuce turned into rotted balls of brown goo. Instead of normally throwing these out, Chef Lemieux said to retrieve them and wash them off. Sure enough, washing these brown balls off revealed a smaller head of lettuce that was still good inside. They were green and fresh and still edible, sort of. They were used in the last salads. Once the fresh veggies were consumed, the crew turned to frozen and canned vegetables.

Breakfast service started in the early morning hours, a walk-in, first come-first served basis. Individual breakfast orders were filled when the cook received the written order on a paper chit. Your order was delivered to the table when ready at the pick-up window. My all time breakfast-hero was Harry Dirks. Harry ate his favorite one main meal a day, and that was breakfast, showing up every morning without fail, to eat his standard "twelve eggs, over easy." The fried eggs were plated on top of one another, to save space on the plate. Along with this, his appetite included ham, bacon, sausage, hash browns, french toast, corned beef hash, pancakes with syrup, and sweet rolls to fill his bottomless pit. Harry ate whatever was being served for breakfast. Two plates were normally used to fill his breakfast order. He showed up early to place his order realizing his order would fill up the majority of the grill space. He didn't want to cause any hold up in the line behind him. Harry's breakfast was delivered to him all at the same time. I remember the food inventory was taken before the start of the patrol. The egg count in the walk-in was fifty-two cases, ten flats of eggs to a case. I believe Harry, with his suitcase sized stomach, ate most of the egg inventory. What was amazing, Harry showed no belly sticking out. He was a lean, 6' 5" in height, head tilted forward, the top of his head barely scraped the overhead as he moved through the boat. He was polite and used table manners, a rare quality among the masses. Harry was a First Class Quartermaster and worked as a Navigator. His job was plotting the ship's courses through out the patrol, plus plotting war games as part of drills for the crew. I can only assume that Harry Dirks slept in a comatose state to digest all that food he ate for breakfast. During the patrol, I never saw him after breakfast. Was this proof that Harry must have been in a state of extended hibernation?

THE ART OF FLUSHING ~

Our submarine tour continues into the bathroom facilities, a popular place visited by 140 men daily. The crew's heads (bathrooms) are located in the Lower Level Operations Compartment. Both are situated port and starboard of the passageway, a main intersection in (LLO) Lower Lever Operations. Forward of this intersection is the crews berthing quarters (a dark area full of sleepers). Aft is a passageway leading to (MCC) Missile Control Center. Located in between is the crews lounge, and beyond it through a door, is the crews' library. There is also a wide staircase leading up to the galley deck and another staircase directly above it leading to the Control Room. The port head has three toilet stalls and three sinks. The starboard head has two toilet stalls, one sink, and two showers.

The process of flushing the toilet (the Thunder-mug) requires some skill and finesse. Hand-eye co-ordination is needed, especially when groggy, returning from periscope depth as Planesmen, or those just awakening from berthing. When you're finished doing your business, you're standing there facing the toilet. The flushing process begins as you reach up and turn the green round knob mounted on the upper right back wall. This allows sea water to flow into the stainless steel toilet. Simultaneously, you pull down the long flushing handle mounted at the base of the toilet. This action rotates a ball-valve which allows the contents in the toilet to drop into the sanitary tank below, flow enough water to wash down the contents, then return the long handle to the shut position. Be sure to leave a water seal. This will prevent the sewer gases from leaking out. Mission accomplished..."Toilet Flushing 101" is an easy process.

All toilet contents flush into "Sanitary Tank #1." When the tank is filled, (it holds approximately 350 gallons of residual byproducts identified as "poop") it's blown to sea and not pumped, because of the solid-byproducts. High pressure air snakes its way through the system to blow the "poop" out to sea. The system is a sealed operation. High pressure air is blown in, "poop" is blown out. It's a simple process unless there are accidental openings in the sealed system during the blowing process.

Imagine if there were unknown openings. This would create an ugly backfire of contents blown upwards into the space from where the open breach occurred. Mostly, all open breaches are caused by human error. "Sanitary one" fills up every 3-4 days. The other sanitary tank is basically for holding grey water received from the galley sinks, crew's sinks, showers, and other areas of draining. The contents of Sanitary two is pumped to sea when full, and is much larger and holds more water due to its greater volume.

However, during each patrol, it seems like someone gets caught misusing the head during the blowing evolution, such as the Sleepy Pee'r. It all starts when he wakes up and rushes to relieve himself, totally oblivious to the warning sign hanging on the door handle, or even the stall he is using. What happens next when the sanitary tank reaches the full mark? As mentioned, it is blown to sea.

Prior to blowing the sanitary tank, the auxiliary man hangs large signs onto the handle of each toilet stall. These are black metal signs with big white letters reading: "BLOWING SANITARY."…It is a fair warning to all. You can't miss them, unless groggy. There are consequences for missing the warning. Several gallons of byproduct will back-fire through the breached opening at super-jet speed if you pull down on that long flushing-handle during the blow cycle. Even if you accidentally fuck up to realize your mistake, even within that split-second, any attempt to reset the flushing handle (shut the opening) is too late. You'll get pummeled by a shit storm, complete with chunky sprinkles. You'll be in shock covered with exploded poop in total disbelief you just decorated yourself.

It's difficult to understand that an accidental opening of the flushing handle, even opened for a only second or two, then immediately shut, can create so much noise as well. But there is a thunderous sound of rippling sheet metal that reverberates throughout the boat, followed by a loud yell, with someone grumbling, "GOD DAMN IT - MOTHER FUCKER - SHIT." The loud noise and cussing travels two decks up to the Control Room where it is heard by all. Without hesitation it grabs everyone's attention, followed by smiles of curiosity, then laughter. Then, there's a mad dash down to the head to see who coronated himself in shit.

Poor, J.B. is witnessed diving into the nearest shower. Curious onlookers gather at the site and stare up at the point of impact. They see a threatening thingamabob stuck to the overhead surrounded by dark sprinkles. Looks like some kind of abstract art launched from the direction of the toilet. It looks wet and nasty. A closer look reveals that it's dripping! The onlookers scatter to take cover. They're creeped-out from what they see. It's not something easily forgotten.

J.B. was not a near miss, but a direct hit, a victim of his own doing. The space surely required a spring cleaning anyway. J.B. was the self-proclaimed, designated super-duper pooper-scooper, and the one-man cleanup crew. J.B.'s work had just begun, starting with scraping off the scary-stuff from the overhead. This is followed by a thorough scrubbing and washing of the entire space with the use of a garden hose and nozzle. A special decontamination soap with elbow grease is applied. All is washed away into the floor drains. The area is squeegeed and hand wiped, similar to an indoor car wash. The head is temporarily closed for cleaning.

The incident creates more than just fun for the crew, it's an unexpected morale booster that breaks up monotonous routines. Awakening the crew's morale with an uncommon event such as this, is a good thing! "We'll gladly take a change in any form that comes our way," even from a "toilet gone wild." J.B. was our hero of the day and even made the headlines in the following morning newspaper. The story appears as, "The Stunt of the Day." J.B. receives some earsplitting commentary as cheers and razing follow him throughout the boat next day. Getting attacked by a "belching Thunder-mug" could happen to any of us. Exercising caution to stay alert, is part of living in a world of continuous adaptations. "Life aboard a submarine can be full of unknown surprises." It can only raise the question of who's next?

INSIGHT OF PHYSICAL SPACE ~

The purpose of the FBM mission is to stay hidden and undetected. The outside world doesn't even know we exist. There are no liberty calls at foreign ports like other submarines. FBMs do not surface for the entire extent of their mission. FBM crews are subject to the confines of a steel tube and all that comes with receiving zero liberty. The nature of our secret operations dictates this, that we are alone and cut off from a normal existence. But we are allowed to receive and send up to twenty-eight words limited radio grams (periods of sending and receiving personal messages) to keep in contact with family or friends. But it certainly doesn't replace having liberty.

FBMs are basically self-sustaining. We have food, water, and air to breathe. The weakest link in submarine operations would be the mental status of the crew. By observing the crew, I have already spotted a few candidates that posses mental deficiencies (goofy-oddball-types) and would fall into the category of the "weakest link." So, there is some truth behind that finding.

The thought of having a taste of a real piece of civilian life would be great for the mental and morale status of the crew. Having that liberty would fill the void. Just one stop in a safe zone would be a positive gesture, as personal space with privacy doesn't exist. The side effects of not having liberty range from a dampening of the crew's morale, to mental stagnation and even depression if you allow it. But, being pushed to the edge of claustrophobia is seldom an issue. Many of the crew overeat and oversleep to deal with these issues, either of which are not healthy options. Currently, physical space overall in a submarine is best described as an existence in a "canned rat maze." Can the size of the can be enlarged?

Comments by others in the sub service laced with teasing and jealousy, jokingly refer to a Boomer (an FBM) as a "floating hotel." After five patrols on the Grant, it's anything but a "floating hotel." Federal prisoners have more physical space and freedom than us, and they're the bad guys. Life aboard a Boomer offers a little more elbowroom than a standard nuclear fast attack sub. There's a striking difference in size when compared to a fast attack type of submarine. Ours is definitely longer in appearance because of the longer missile (approx.125' longer) compartment that was added later, to convert it to an FBM. This was an added feature: By fitting the missile compart-ment in the middle of the boat after cutting a fast attack submarine in half, you get a boomer. Adopting the name of "floating hotel" gives a false impression. However, the new longer look of the FBM could be mistaken as a nickname, "The U.S.S. John Holmes" of the submarine fleet. John Holmes was a famous porno star for possessing "a much longer unit," which could be mistaken as his own personal missile.

FBMs are mainly designed for the functionality of their war deliv-ery systems and not intended for the mental health needs of the crew. The crew could use more space for physical relaxation and mental balance, but space defines reality. As before mentioned, the crew's lack of mental stability is the weakest link of the crew, and could be tested during an unplanned extended time at sea. It is rumored, studies have been conducted by professionals regarding this very subject. Protect-ing the crew from any hint of claustrophobic (or other confinement) concerns should have been a vital focus when incorporated into the overall submarine design. A design feature offering more room for the crew is missing, space is sacrificed for speed.

A solution regarding this dilemma, would be possibly adding a third crew to the existing schedule. The FBM would have three crews, instead of just two. The FBM schedule would then look something like 3 months out to sea and 6 months in for R&R. This would be a compensating factor in allowing the crew to spend twice the time with rest and relaxation. The crew can look forward to this extended time off, away from the sub, and an extra long period to enjoy the real world. Adding that third R (Recovery) would buttress the Rest, Relaxation and would be a big part of the plan. Natural sunshine and fresh air can do wonders in rebuilding normalcy to the human spirit, and for those who need a lengthier period to deal with their mental-repairs. However, neither option seems practical in terms of navy thinking. (A larger paycheck would serve as an ample incentive).

The downside of this "wishful thinking" would mean increasing by thirty percent the current FBM operational population. There are currently forty-one FBMs (in the 1960's). This possible solution would be counterproductive in terms of naval spending, but it would be the saving grace in better treatment of the sub crew members. Towards the end of my four year tour, a new generation of submarines was being developed. It was the end of the FBM era. They were sent to the shipyards to be refitted as "Trident Submarines." Hopefully, the new designs of future replacement subs were roomier with additional interior space. Currently, the lower level missile compartment on some FBMs was used for exercise, jogging, and a few outdated weight machines. This space was really not adequate, being placed there only as an after thought. It was not popular with the crew and seldom used. Conversely, more eating and sleeping would take precedence over burning off those stored calories.

CLAUSTROPHOBIA ~

Your existence is cramped, but not too close to claustrophobic. You can become claustrophobic if you allow your imagination to drift into the dark side, and to allow the feeling of impending doom with the walls closing in. Dwelling on your cramped existence is not good for the morale. In order to feel better, just think about the confines of tank cleaning? As an example and contrast, picture yourself being stuck inside to scrape the byproducts from a sanitary tank. You're scraping all six sides of 8" thick gunk, then hauling it out through a hatch. It is work that is stifling hot, dingy, gross, and cramped. You're wearing a gas mask for protection. That certainly can add to your confinement fears. And your body is in a small confined space, surrounded in shit. What could be a better condition for getting claustrophobia?

In comparison to living in a rat maze, submarine duty is much easier to deal with. This roomier contrast can even make you feel better. Sometimes it is just a matter of accepting the fact that you are stuck here for a short time. It is very academic, a very black and white reality. Wrap your mind around it and go with it! There is nothing but your point of view you can change about it anyway.

Sometimes you'll stop and ask yourself, "what am I doing here?" This is the life you chose when you signed up volunteering for sub duty. Good luck, if you have regrets about it. If you can't stand it, chalk it up as another bad choice in life. There is no un-volunteering at sea. The upside of the submarine experience can be viewed as good character building, and can be added to your life's contributing core of finer things. For a quick remedy, go to bed and dream about getting "lost in space." As previously mentioned, having a talk with that familiar face in the mirror while shaving is another sounding board. Give him some sympathy while having that talk, if that works? Think of it in these terms and claustrophobia doesn't stand a chance invading your being. There is always the choice of getting a "professional head adjustment" at the end of patrol. Meanwhile, pretend you're an astronaut floating in space. This will ground your brain, tricking it into thinking you're not claustrophobic. Besides, it's too late to show concern about the subject. You're just another rat ricocheting off the walls in this underwater paradise, if you are so inclined. If you slipped through the cracks of the weeding out process, you shouldn't have made it this far into subs. I never witnessed any panic attacks indicating claustrophobia during my five patrols on the Grant. Claustrophobia remains a moot subject.

Submarine duty could be viewed as being a castaway into solitude. Scratch your way out by eating, sleeping, or standing watch is a boring scenario of repetition. There are not many exciting nor personal options to occupy the time. The time will pass whether or not you participate in it. An "all hands on deck drill" thrown into the mix, or a "field day" of deep cleaning the boat helps break-up the hum drum day and refreshes the air. These are temporary fixes. Developing habits of reading paperback books in the library, board games, poker, or other card games are options too. Learning the game of chess, cribbage, or bridge could be a challenging mental exercise. Readdressing your energy. Not only gets you involved with the challenge, but given enough time you'll become a skilled opponent. Playing games could perk your interest. Jump with both feet into something you absolutely know nothing about. To develop skills on the subject is something to look forward to. Find and use some self-help techniques to occupy your mind. Finding a teammate to take on the rest of the boat by entering a posted contest would help fill the time of the patrol. These are some suggestions to expand and jumpstart your brain.

Change your interest just by refocusing your priority. But, they may not jive with your personality profile. Sitting in a dark corner knitting a sweater maybe your style. Whatever works...or continue sleeping it off. Occupying your mind is a healthy distraction while holding claustrophobia at bay. There are no head-adjustment counselors aboard, except for yourself.

LIVING SUB LIFE IN STYLE ~

Officer's quarters is located in the mid level Operations Compartment which is located forward of the Control Room. The Captain has his living quarters located here near all of the action and forward of the Control Room which is past the radio shack and sonar room. The Control Room is the "Nerve Center" of the sub. The status of the boat's depth, speed, course, and maneuvering is monitored and directed from here. The Captain needs to be near this space. The officers have access to their own private wardroom (basically an upscale roomy lounge). It's a relatively large and plush space for taking their meals, for their regular meetings, and for relaxation. They also have separate and private living quarters. The officers share a two men per cabin living space, which is much larger for storage of their personal stuff. Their own private head is also contained within their quarters.

The officers are spoiled, having a fairly luxurious arrangement. Their everyday needs are at their disposal. Finger snapping is not necessary for immediate service. They have immediate access to the Filipino servants who tend to their needs and cleanup after them, shine their shoes, care for their laundry, make their beds, etc. Let's face it, the officers are spoiled sub-brats. The Filipino personnel are their janitors, house maids, butlers, and waiters, all rolled up into one. The only commonality with the officers and the enlisted crew is that we eat the same meals, prepared by the same cooks, and served out of the same galley. However, the officers are served by Filipino waiters, using linen napkins, table linens, china, and silver flatware with complete silver service. Maybe this is what is meant in referencing a "floating hotel." But, officers or enlisted, we're all rats trapped in the same damn can.

SAILORS AS SERVANTS ~

A small area of the boat is occupied by a Filipino staff. They are designated members of the navy. Their sole purpose on the sub is to serve and tend to the needs of the officers. Good attitudes and showing gratitude having this job is prevalent with them. No complaints are heard, even though they are not allowed to wander about the boat. They are restricted to the Operation Compartment, the forward part of the boat within a three deck existent. They are not a "vital functioning" part of the submarine operations, other than their designated limited servant jobs. These "servants for the officers" are not qualified as submarine personnel and they are not required to be. The Filipinos do not have a secret clearance and therefore do not have "a need to know." They bunk with the rest of the crew in Lower Level Operations Compartment (LLOPS). And, they go to the mess hall and kitchen areas when required. The Filipinos keep to themselves, by speaking their foreign language. Danny (Chief Commissary man) is the head Filipino, and their leader of the group. He is assigned to keeping the food inventory on the boat, and he is also the head-chief cook in the main galley. He is in charge of the entire cooking staff of the Grant. Only the supply officer is above him in rank. He is responsible for moving the food service from the galley into the wardroom (the officer's dining room). The Filipino staff present the food and serve it to the officers as though they were dining in a first class restaurant (complete with trained waiters, dressed in white formal jackets, and plates dressed with garnishes for a formal appearance). The Filipino staff truly exist in a life of confinement due to their limited function and limited freedom of movement about the boat. They are considered heroes by their families for the money they send back home to the Philippines.

THE GOAT LOCKER ~

The chiefs on board the Grant reside in their private living quarters called the "Goat Locker." It's quite a contrast to the living spaces of the officers. This next section is appropriately mentioned just for them. The space is contaminated by a ghastly aroma. It's a cross between smelly people and the essence of farm animals.

At the top of the smelling chart is the goat. The odor is so thick, you can cut it with a knife; and it's a sure measure in challenging your gag reflex. All non-quals should be introduced to this area, just to add some stress to what lies ahead. The door to the Goat locker should be marked with the appropriate "skull and cross bones" as a warning to those when entering or another that would read: " Your life is at risk if your breathe behind this door." A spray to neutralize the odor with a auto-mister dispenser would be nice to cover the smell of decomposition. Otherwise, a breathing rag, doused with your favorite cologne, covering your noise and mouth, is a good life saver.

The chiefs of each department sleep here (the most senior of enlisted personnel). This is their berthing area. Contained within their space are their racks, smells, and lockers. There is a small lounge area consisting of a table and chairs located forward of their personal zone. There are approximately 8 to 10 goats here. The air in there is the foulest I have ever breathed. I had to enter the area on a few occasions. I can remember almost passing-out from holding my breath for so long. (Wearing a gas mask would have gotten some laughs). Thank God their area is situated apart from the remainder of the crew, otherwise drifting vapors would kill us all in our sleep. Fumes in their space have the propensity for peeling paint from the walls. The door to their quarters was located across and aft of the galley and crew's mess. The first dining table when you entered the mess area was designated for chiefs only. Probably, no one wanted to sit next to them. Obviously soap and water was absent from their daily sanitation agenda. If smell had a color, it would most likely be a putrid green.

One of the goats showed up at his watch station as the diving officer in the Control Room. His station (chair) is located behind the planesmen. This is his spot for the next 6 hours. He seemed fiercely pissed off for some reason. He was mumbling that someone laced his bed sheets with finely ground sawdust particles. Finely ground salt is also a good attention grabber. Just a small sprinkle will do its magic. Sugar will also do the same and maybe sweeten the situation. Imagine, trying to sleep with that in your sheets. Perhaps, someone was sending a message to wash the bedding too. Clean up guys! You're giving sub sailors a bad name.

WHERE WE LIVE ~

The enlisted crew mainly survive and live in the Lower Level Operations Compartment. Other than standing their watch station, this area is where life happens for the crew. Crews berthing is located here. The berthing area is configured like two letter H's joined together. This area is kept in the dark around the clock, except during drills and field days when the lights are on. It's our sleeping quarters. There is a lack of ambient lighting, and you must rely on a memorized roadmap in your mind, in order to maneuver in the dark. These are narrow hallways lined with racks (beds) and small personal lockers next to them. Racks and lockers line both sides of the hallways. The racks are stacked three high, one above of the other. The corresponding lockers are stacked, located at the head side of each rack. Every one has his own rack and locker. The racks are orientated with head and foot positioned to the forward and aft of the boat. There is no "hot bunking," that is, no sharing of beds like the past sub operations. The racks are no longer than 6 foot in length, and barely shoulder width (2 1/2 feet). Dirks had to sleep fetal like. If you're over six foot tall, you get to sleep in the semi-fetal position. They are built against a wall and the locker is also built-in for maximum usage of space. Getting into your rack requires "slipping-in" using a slithering-in method. There's not much clearance space for height. The guy on top needs to use the lower racks as a step ladder to climb up. Each rack area has a short curtain that can be drawn when sleeping and there is also a small bunk light for reading. If you raise your head up 6-8 inches, you risk banging your head on the light.

Problems arise during emergencies or drills. When the trip-lights come on, an audible alarm is sounded, followed by a verbal announcement. Everyone bails out of the rack at the same time. Remember, we're sleeping stacked three high as in a triple bunk bed. Quickly sliding out from hibernation mode and bumping the guy below is a common occurrence. It can't be avoided. You're half asleep. The guy sleeping on the bottom rack gets pulverized most often. He needs to be aware of falling bodies from above, or to be last out. When you're sleeping, little nuances of any noise are disturbing. Yet, the noise that blows in from the poker games is mostly tolerated, along with difficulty sleeping through and within this snoring chamber. There are 15 different audible alarms to be interpreted while bailing out of the rack. The audible alarms indicate where to report to for an emergency (a prearranged reporting location, subject to change, depending on which drill you are responding to). Being half asleep, confusion is a common occurrence remembering where to report.

There is no talking allowed down here. Even whispering can awaken the sleepers. Nasty comments will be heard from "disturbed-light sleepers" when this occurs. Crew's berthing is considered a sacred zone for silence. Any noise can irritate those sleeping such as a mess cook removing the deck plates searching for food. Some simple things can't be avoided. Near the end of each shift, the off-going seaman comes down to berthing and wakes up the on coming shift. This is done by finding 20-30 fast asleep sailors and physically shaking them and telling them it's time to get up. Using the verbal wake ups along with shaking is a dangerous maneuver. Sometimes the sleeper will swing his fist at you followed by a few nasty choice words. Even in the dark, you can feel the air move past your face from a fast moving fist. Waking up the on coming shift can be hazardous. The designated seaman doing his job becomes a moving target. He needs to locate the correct sleeper with a name on a clip board and with a berthing diagram using a red-lensed flashlight to awaken him. He shines the light on the locker for the name, and in his face to get him up. This usually pisses him off. You have to be constantly on guard, ready to dodge flying fists, accompanied with a few choice cuss words. There is no quiet way of doing this, so it often awakens other sleepers nearby. It usually requires two visits per wake up call. The off-going person can be so angry when his relief shows up late. I made sure my relief was on time. My watch station as helmsman, was 6 hours on and 12 hours off. My day was calculated as an 18 hour day and time passes slowly on this schedule. It seems to foreshorten a 24 hour day, that easily stretches time of the patrol. Every third day, you serve the 1st and 4th watches. It's a 18 hour day no matter how you slice it.

Other schedules vary, so there were constant noises causing disruptions during sleeping. Quality sleep was non-existent for the most part. But, the Dr. had drugs if needed. Job burnout is a result of being tired, irritated, and could be laced with a touch of depression. Of course, there are those who can sleep through anything, the lucky few. The atmosphere in berthing can be a good training ground for human behavior. You never know what you'll run into when roving through the maze of dark passageways of a submarine. Wearing a plexiglass face shield for making wake up calls should be required as standard protocol. I have experienced too many close connections while wandering in the dark. I was lucky to escape unscathed during those many wake-up calls.

WAKING UP MY RELIEF ~

When I had the duty of waking up the oncoming shift, I paid special attention to my relief to make sure he was on time. He slept on the bottom rack near the entrance to berthing, and easy to locate. I brought him a hot cup of coffee, placed it on his chest, and carefully put both of his hands around the cup to steady it from getting spilled. Then I tapped him on the shoulder. I found this method was an effective way of awakening my relief, a kinder way of getting him up. Everything went well until one morning shift. I placed the coffee on his chest, and at that exact moment, the missile jettison alarm went off. My relief, startled by the alarm, raised up in a flash, spilling hot coffee on himself while simultaneously banging his head on the bunk light. The two sleepers above him, baled out and landed on him, almost hitting me. Blame it on the untimely drill that caused the mishap, or me. My relief (Pete), unfortunately started with a scorching-bad day. He said that he would pass on any future wake up calls involving hot coffee deliveries.

During another wake up session, Pete didn't respond. Several attempts were made to shake him awake. In the past few days Pete had been working at a rampaging pace to get ahead in his quals. This attributed to his apparent exhaustion. A decision was made to let him sleep it off. He was dead to the world and vital signs were checked. Pete was still with us, just worn out and unconscious, escaping into a deep sleep. Someone put the clock on him. He slept straight threw for 2 days, non- stop. We covered his shifts. It was a good run for snoozing, as a new record was set aboard the Grant. The crew monitored him, making sure he was still alive. Finally, he "failed open," (a sub term indicating, you're slept out). Upon awakening, Pete thought he was late for watch. He was clued-in regarding his vegetative state. It kept him from having any stress attacks. It was evident that being short on sleep can contribute to the zombie mental state most submariners have experienced. It's an unsafe condition. But, 50 years ago, who knew, and who even cared? Submariner behavior, and tracking statistics were still pretty new in the late 60's. No one tracked or cared about the data regarding the dynamics of the human condition, after you made the cut.

COFFEE RUNNERS ~

Sometimes the morning shift in the Control Room was an unpleasant place to work, all because of the demands of one particular Diving Chief. He turns into an "Irritant" when he is on duty, and earns that name. His dislikable nature seemed to be deep seated. The Diving Chief is perched and seated behind the two Planesmen which is his spot for the entire shift. The Diving Chief receives his orders from the Conning Officer, Officer of the Deck, also known as the OD (officer of the deck, on duty) and passes any changes of depth, course, and trim adjustments to the Planesmen via the Diving Chief. The Diving Chief can also give orders to the (BCP Operator) Ballast Control Panel Operator, via the Conning Officer. Depending on the mood of the Diving Chief, he can screw you over when he's in a bad mood. He'll keep the boat in a "manual maneuvering" mode, to overwork the Planesmen. This was totally unnecessary and requires total concentration for controlling the submarine. It adds stress to the Planesmen while trying to keep the boat's depth and bubble from oscillating too much. The hand-eye- co-ordination and quick adjustment movements can wear out the Planesmen during his six hour shift. Both Planesmen on duty can rotate their positions during their 6 hour shift (one Planesman operates the fairwater planes, the other operates the stern planes and the rudder). The "Irritant" can easily switch out of manual maneuvering control, using his own discretion, and into automatic maneuvering control (AMC) which is preferred by the Planesmen. However, at the very start of the shift, the Irritant begins whining about needing his morning coffee. He should stop by the galley to bring his own coffee like anyone else. Besides, it's on the way to the Control Room. Not all Diving Chiefs are "Irritants." Of the five chiefs, he's the only one that complains. The others make an effort to bring their own coffee.

There is no easy way of making coffee deliveries to those in the Control Room. The Diving Chief is always sending one of the Planesmen down to the galley to help fetch everyone's coffee. I usually completed the task in one trip. The Planesmen are used by the "Irritant" and are ordered about as his personal coffee waiters. One shift, I asked the OD if I could borrow one of the Filipinos to fetch the coffee order this time. I purposely said it in a loud voice to piss-off the "Irritant," and it apparently did. Hearing my comment that was intended jokingly, I sensed he was upset for going over his head. The OD saw the humor in the comment and reacted with a smirk on his face. The Diving Chief's sense of humor fell short and was not fazed by the comment. He reacted by getting meaner during the shift. He was always on the rag, no place for a man's man. This Diving Chief usually insisted on taking coffee orders for everyone. He enjoys exercising his authority over the Planesmen in order to impress the OD. This is how he earned the name "Irritant," being a real pain in the ass.

Coffee orders can consist of blond, blond and sweet, blond and bitter, black, black and bitter, or black and sweet. The coffee order can be as interpreted as a double header, selecting a lady in a brothel or choosing a cup of coffee, or so I'd been told. In order to keep the coffee order straight, I would write it down on a slip of paper. Once the coffee order is made up and ready to be brought from the galley to the Control Room, negotiating the side to side swaying during the one flight up stairway can be a problem. Coffee cups are stacked, one on top of the other, which requires perfect balance when carrying. (Handles on the cups are used for carrying, not a tray). Usually, two trips are made to get the job done. Sometimes several coffee runs are made during the 6 hour shift, that requires wiping up some minor spills. Coffee orders and deliveries can be a long process. Our time could be better spent as Planesmen, not as hot coffee delivery boys.

One morning I was the designated coffee gopher. As a courtesy to the Diving Chief, I mentioned that the coffee maker was recently returned from a thorough disassembly and cleaning. It was temporarily out of commission. Recently, there had been too many complaints from the crew about the coffee tasting bad. It was foul tasting. A higher up decision was made to give the maker a thorough cleaning. The guys in the machinery spaces were assigned to clean it up, then reinstall it in brand new condition. The coffee maker had not been properly cleaned since its installation years ago. This was a major task. The commercial coffee maker was missing for three days while being overhauled back aft. It was a serious cleanup. It involved breaking down the monstrous coffee maker to include every nut, bolt, and screw. I learned that lubricants and other unknown cleaners were used in the disassembly and during the cleaning. I iterated that "lingering residue still might be present which could possibly taint the coffee. It may taste like coffee, but beware. Laxative effects could be lurking in the brew."

I gave a fair word of caution to those who were considering drinking the coffee; and it was my last. Of course, the "Irritant" made his own assessment that trumped my warning, ignoring anything I said. He knew about all that stuff. In spite of that, he was in a rush to be the first to taste the fresh brewed coffee. The re-installation of the coffee maker was finished just minutes before starting our shift in the Control Room. Tired of drinking instant coffee, he called Danny insisting on a new batch of coffee, immediately. Danny insisted "the coffee maker first needs another thorough flushing." In spite of that warning, the "Irritant" wanted his damned coffee now and that was his final word. So, I reiterated a final suggestion to stick with instant a bit longer. He said, "just bring it gopher!"

I was anticipating the results of my forewarned-prediction for those drinking the coffee too soon after cleaning. I drank tea that morning. The Diving Chief's poor judgement could backfire on him, and may end up in his shorts. He never, to my knowledge, passed on any of this information to the others in the Control Room. So, to be fair to everyone, upon delivering the coffee, I made a final verbal announcement to everyone. Following the warning, I kept my mouth shut. I was thinking….good-luck to everyone. I was definitely tired of the "Irritant's" cavalier attitude. He was the instigator in the Control Room, attempting to influence others to follow his lead. When I was the chosen runner, I liked fixing their coffee, just as I was told. This required a few extra minutes in careful preparation of the coffee order. The delay got him mad, as I took notes for accuracy. I only did this so as not to mix up the order. Oh yeah, and to piss him off.

After making the delivery, everyone drank the coffee, and no complaints were made. "I told you so, good stuff!," said the "Irritant," spouting off, looking for approval. It was amazing that some taste-less, odorless, and not so harmless residue can be transferred to the coffee. Nothing occurred immediately, but as time passed, there was rumbling and a rude awakening. Those who drank the coffee couldn't trust their "thunder down under." Holding back an urge to go was not an option any longer. Then, the "Irritant," was soon hit with "the dance of the flaming sphincter" (otherwise known as the hot-squirts). Many trips were made to the head by those who chose to imbibe the new and freshly brewed java. Pretty soon, all were affected by the scourge of "Colonic Purification."

It's amazing how a change of events can pop up out of thin air. The Planesmen always caught their unfair share of flack and ridicule by the "Irritant." When the coffee incident came up, it ushered in a reversal of changes, as the Control Room was hit by the unexpected surprise. Ingesting the fresh brewed coffee, just as the "Irritant" insist-ed, became an unanticipated stunner to him when he disregarded my previous, multiple warnings.

I had a hunch of what was coming. I sat back to watch the others move at warp speed, taking turns to quickly relocate with their appointed destiny, the toilet. All the while, attempting to keep their orifices pinched tightly-shut. The stairs, having a close proximity to the fairwater planes, was in plain view. Nothing was missed. I've never seen so many move so fast. And I acknowledged their presence as they raced passed. "Slow down! Don't trip on the way down" I muttered to the "Irritant" as he hustled by me. Then, I said: Where are you going again?, just to get my message across. Throughout the shift, those who drank the questionable fresh brew, were having second thoughts about drinking the coffee. It was certainly too late. More importantly, I suggested that they needed a visit to see Doc to deal with their colon-blow. It is noted: "A word to the wise is sufficient. A word to a sailor is pointless." You get the point.

Apparently, the coffee also worked as a handy relief for "hung-chow," a Chinese remedy for constipation. This morning, the Control Room underwent a mysterious metamorphosis, causing it to lose control. I'd never witnessed so much movement in the Control Room shortly after starting the shift that morning. It was a refreshing experience to view things differently. I quietly smiled at what was taking place. It definitely taught the "Irritant" that insisting on getting your own way, isn't always the best option. The morning event put me in a good mood. I thought about sharing some freshly brewed java with Mr. Happy. Perhaps, the fresh java will help flush away his "angry spirits." Most likely, three visits to the head will help cure his problem.

BACK TO GUAM ~

It was late one Summer and we were returning to Guam to catch our sub. We flew Braniff Airlines. Our crew traveled by unannounced and secret schedules to and from Guam where our boat was located. Yet, everyone seemed to know about them. So much for secret flights. When we landed, I noticed all of the blankets were taken by the crew as we deplaned. The stewardesses in the cabin said nothing, as they expected and planned for it. This was probably a ritual and a common practice each flight. I knew something was up, as there was a blanket shortage on the sub and the boat was freezing cold. Later I discovered the smaller size blankets fit our sub racks perfectly. The stewardess told our crew we could take them. I left mine behind, having missed the message.

Our sub was moored to the sub tender when we arrived. Another Boomer, the "Andrew Jackson" was tied up on the opposite side. Our crew was buried in four days of busy maintenance and loading stores, missiles, torpedoes, assorted supplies, and ancillary spare parts. All were supplied from the sub tender. It was all hands on deck involvement. This was our daily routine while tied up. Other jobs were prepping and painting rust spots, scraping the crud from inside the tanks, including the sea crud from under the top-side superstructure. The smelly seaweed and dead sea organisms stuck in your nose all day. Our crew couldn't wait to get back out at sea and settle down to a normal routine. The zinc plates that reacted with the sea water to preserve the hull were also checked and replaced as needed in the superstructure.

Andy's Hut, a local dive bar and permanent fixture, was just a short stroll away, maybe 300 yards inland. This was the sub crew's nighty hangout and place of release after work, plus it was the only local business within walking distance. The bar featured canned Olympia beer laced with formaldehyde. The luxurious ingredient, commonly known as embalming fluid, was added to the beer for preservation and gave the beer a horrible taste. It was the standard offering, and unfortunately, the only beer in town. The beer was barely cool, and my shipmates drank a lot of it. I stayed away from it, but it was the last push for the crew to entertain themselves at Andy's hut. It was all about drinking in excess at the last close-by, cheap, beer on earth. Getting drunk, and to ready themselves for the upcoming patrol, was paramount to all else. Sailors gathered here to reminisce and share tales over the blaring out dated music from the jukebox. It was the last chance fill-up station for booze before heading out, and getting lost at sea for a few months.

The weather on Guam was always partly cloudy, with hot sizzling temperatures, soaking humidity, and off and on, pouring rain showers. The air in Guam was stifling, heavy and hard to breath. I stayed on the boat surrounded in the A.C. as much as I could. When you left the boat, you crossed the gangway that was connected the sub tender. After crossing the sub tender, another gangway connected you to shore. I distinctly experienced a sudden rain shower crossing the tender. It was a sharp line of demarcation divided by a single step of distance. One step forward, without warning, I was in pouring rain. One step back, I was out of the rain. It was so strange, I did it again to just make sure. I looked up to check for an end of an overhead covering. There was none, including zero wind. I realized that I had walked through the edge of a rain curtain. It was a strange occurrence and never happened again. Nature unique to Guam, what crazy weather there.

The topside security watch was stationed topside to greet you upon your return to the boat. One day we flunked our security test. An unknown person slipped by the watch onto the boat. Topside activities are full of distractions. I could see how someone could slip past the security watch. The incident didn't occur on my watch. The Captain got upset. What took place was, an unknown person entered below decks carrying a cardboard box. On the box was the word "Bomb," clearly printed in large letters. Four hours later an alert crewman finally noticed the box and bomb. He turned him in. So much for our security and the lack of it. Mishaps and misjudgments regarding security could occur even back then. Security measures can be breached anytime, anywhere, by anyone. Even today, there are holes in many facets of security, everywhere offering opportunities for would be terrorists.

The topside watch assignments were held by the lower ranking members of the crew. Two topside security guards stood the four hour watch around the clock while tied to the Proteus (the submarine tender). We were packing .45 caliber sidearms. Duties are to check IDs of everyone coming aboard including those sailors returning from Andy's

Hut. After the cardboard box-bomb incident, a message was sent from the Captain for the top-side watch to do their jobs more efficiently. I was looking for the "Irritant" to pass my topside watch station so I could goose his "huevos rancheros" during a pat down. Of course, just to send him a message that I was complying with the Captain's orders. It didn't happen damn it. He never passed by. It's amazing how the Guamanian humidity does kooky things to your thoughts.

Many of the returnees from Andy's Hut were "drunk on their asses." It was part of their every evening drinking ritual. Drinking to get thoroughly drunk, was their mission before returning to sea. It was their final opportunity to drink in excess, to binge in consuming tomorrow's alcoholic beverages before cutting themselves completely off. Being drunk, and not having a serious care in the world for the next sixty-five days was the point. For some, it was a sad day. They weren't looking forward to the return at a long dry period. It was their last affair with booze and beer. For a while now, it's preparation for another outing at sea. Some of the crew, upon returning to the boat, just slid down the forward hatch without setting a foot on the ladder rungs on the way down. Using the hand rails only, it was amazing to watch as there were no broken ankles when they hit deck. They went straight to bed or stopped by the galley for a mid-night snack and then poured themselves into their racks.

However, during the late evening hours, two familiar drinking buddies were always seen together. Sitting far apart and arguing using the foulest language. They sat in the empty galley venting their beer laced anger. I witnessed a flying glass jar of sugar just missing someone's head and smashing into the bulkhead. It was a near nightly drunken argument. It became a regular event between the two. I've seen plenty of those. They were unruly, drunken, and "just unwinding," as they say. Witnessing these drunken sailors met the typical navy stereotype. On another time there was a big gathering of sailors outside of Andy's Hut. I went over to see what was happening. It was loud. I thought it was a major fight brewing.

Another FBM was tied up to the other side of the sub tender. This meant twice the loitering and drunken sailors at Andy's Hut. The Hut was packed to the gills. The extra number of sailors that couldn't fit inside were loitering outside surrounding the entrance. I noticed a large crowd was gathering around a drunken sailor. This young kid was so drunk, his friends cut him off. He was upset and wanted more to drink. His friends had already picked him up off the ground twice and then dusted him off. He was leaning on a palm tree for support and kept slipping down it. He was then seen wandering through the crowd, begging for beer money. His shipmates told him to go back to the boat. The kid bet the crowd that he could eat a live frog for five dollars. He had it in his grasp. He was waving it around, showing it off. It was a good thing the frog was small and bite size. Several five dollar bets were made. Everyone grimaced when he bit the head off, then spit it on the ground. He pushed the rest in his mouth. Only the ends of the flippers were sticking out of the corners of his mouth. He grimaced as he swallowed the amphibian snack. He won several five dollar bets, the hard way. But, maybe an easy way for him. The kid scored a quick twenty-five dollars as he collected from the bettors. He pushed his way back inside for a beer to wash down his frog appetizer. It still amazes me what people will do for beer money. That day, a drunken sailor topped the list of weirdest stuff that I've ever witnessed. My observation told me that he must have been very hungry, very thirsty and very crazy.

NO ONE LIKES SEA TRIALS ~

Before we actually began our sixty plus day patrol, we had to undergo "sea trials." "Sea trials" is a short period for testing both the endurance of the crew and the strength of the submarine facing the punishing fury of the mighty Pacific Ocean. We take the boat to sea and give it a short workout to find any discrepancies with the boat and of the crew (mental discrepancies of the crew were excluded). The boat is taken through high speed, angles and dangles, (ups and downs). These gymnastic maneuvers for the boat are made during sea trials only, and are not normally exercised during the patrol. The boat is pushed just hard enough, not enough to break it, but only to keep it within the prescribed "benchmark limitations." The erratic movement was rough enough that some crew members even got sea sick. I remember someone saying, "I thought I lost that three patrols ago." The steep downward angle of the boat shook something loose, hidden in the maze of wiring chase, in the overhead. During these maneuvers, hold onto something or you'll be thrown across the compartment. You can watch shoes in berthing slide up and then down, back and forth. The cooks in the galley were cussing, as their stock pots began spilling over from the sub's steep diving angles. The cooks enraged and pissed off, called upstairs to the Control Room and said: "If you guys want to eat on time, knock the shit-off!!" The boat and crew were taken to their maximum limits, nearly touching the breaking points of both. This 24/7 schedule was a ball breaker and lasted for one or two days. If you're sleeping, sharp angles of the boat allowed your body to slide up and down in your rack. You'll find your head pressed against the wall, and then, your feet get pressed in the opposite direction. You can hear the outside water whooshing by, and the moans and groans of the pressure hull being tweaked and squeezed by sea pressure. Sea trials are filled with constant emergency evolutions provided by the senior staff. This is done to keep the crew on their toes, and alert. During the maneuvers, I felt the boat shutter. That's scary and unnerving, not knowing what caused it.

The second day of sea trials was the worst. The Captain and his officers kept up the routine of taking both man and machine to the edge of failure, but no farther. Whatever the Captain and his officers could drum up to test the crew, occurred. Testing them to the max was the goal. Some drills were put to a maximum time limit, repeating the same drills until they're satisfied. We tested all modes and functions of the boat looking for any leaks during dives, and any other equipment failures or weaknesses. Sea trials, was a required pre-routine, to ready the boat and the 140 men for patrol. Testing included identifying fifteen audible alarms that the crew needed to recognize, then properly react to during any given emergency situation. Confusion, caused by lack of sleep brought on by the relentless series of testing, can expose the crew to some fast developing fatigue. The repetition of these drills can send the crew to the brink of crankiness and craziness. Or for some, to the edge of not giving a damn anymore. Repetition of over-drilling becomes counterproductive.

Not until the Captain is satisfied in punishing the crew with his untimely drills, could we finally return to normal routines; and finally to be left alone in peace. To mark the grueling finish of sea trials, our sub headed back to the sub tender. The end of sea trials marked the beginning of two days of topping-off with stores and an evening beer guzzling marathon at Andy's Hut. The excessive beer drinking was needed to fend off the ravages of sea trials. Once back, it required several days of sleep and recuperation, just to recover from the punishing workout at sea. Then, it was back to sea to start the actual beginning of the patrol.

It was a time for the crew to mellow out and recover from sea trials. For the non-quals, it is just the start of their patrol nightmares. The ravages of sea trials is considered just a warm up period for what lies ahead, as their reputation will be a continuation of the same. It's a nonstop chaotic environment especially designed for the non-quals, enduring many more long hours of grueling work until they get qualified in submarines. It takes two patrols on the Grant to finish sub quals. There is a much needed break in Hawaii, which occurs between the first two patrols at sea. Once the rest and recuperation period ends, the crew will agonize over leaving their relaxing enjoyment and tropical retreat in Hawaii, just to face more of the same hardships that awaits them returning to the Grant. It doesn't seem fair, but the whole crew is subject to the same program of three months of R&R, three months out to sea, which was prescribed throughout the year. For some, it becomes a deja vu time-table to mess with your sanity. The FBM mission is to be at sea full time. It has two crews to fulfill the mission, the blue crew and the gold crew. The switching out period of the two crews allows a dead period of about two weeks. Reloading stores, spare parts, and making minor repairs occurs during that time. It marks the beginning and ending of something both good and bad for each of the crews. For one crew, it's the rebirth of a long awaited vacation in paradise, and for the other, another regretful time returning to sea. Then again, a period before for the visa-versa to come full circle to repeat itself.

SHIPBOARD DRILLS ~

The captain could use a new hobby to occupy his spare time. "Drills and thrills" continued during the normal patrol time, but not as often. Doesn't he remember going through "sea trials at all?" Over drilling is disturbing to the crew, not only does it disturb our peace and quiet, but too much contributes to mental stresses and spoils the morale. Leave us alone. Repetition after a certain point doesn't make us any better, it has the opposite affect, and tends to piss us off. These drills are time consuming and they need to be cleaned up. Later, they are discussed and critiqued.Putting us on a stop watch during the drill doesn't improve the situation. There is a list of drills which requires mostly an all hands on deck participation. Drills can involve the following scenarios: fire, flooding, collision, battle station missile, battle station torpedo, missile jettison, explosion in the machinery space, broaching the boat, losing radio signal, losing electrical power, switching to diesel power, emergency ventilation, emergency diving, emergency blow to the surface, losing ship's propulsion, losing rudder function, losing depth control, losing sonar capabilities, emergency sonar contacts, poison gas release, poisonous gas from the battery well, emergency blow to the surface. This list of time consuming drills must each be practiced. Many drills, evolutions, and scenarios are missing, too many to list but can be created.

These drills can occur at any time during the patrol. Fires and flooding can occur in any compartment. The drills may be moved from one place to another to create new scenarios. The officers running the drills are allowed to take turns, and sometimes they attempt to "out do" one another, at the expense of the crew.

I'm fully aware that the captain was most-likely mandated to achieve certain levels of competence by training to perform at a high level of competence. The officers are just following orders, but their actions need some refinement when implementing. Over-drilling just jerks-off the crew. If it is for the benefit of the junior officers, they should train them before coming aboard, somewhere else off-site to get their thrills. Again, these drills should not be at the expense of the crew.

The fact remains that in a true emergency, depending on the severity of flooding resulting in extensive damage to the boat, including a massive and exhaustive effort to save it, there comes a point of no return. It becomes a bleak scenario of helplessly sinking into the deep ocean abyss without possibility of recovery. It's a chilling end to all life aboard the Grant. Faced with this grim reality, the only course of action that remains is to bend over and kiss your ass good-bye, while whispering that familiar slogan, "Adios Cruel World."

HEAVY SCOPE IN LEARNING ~

Sub quals is an intense and varied curriculum to be learned within a short period of time. The learning curve doesn't exist in the normal sense because it's made up as you move forward in learning. Studying the layers of detailed information can overwhelm the memory capacity. The non-qual is issued a booklet of schematic drawings.

Contained within are all of the boat's twelve systems, plus other ancillary information. After thinking back 50 years, there maybe more, too many to recall. Within each system there are sub-systems. These are complex systems that would rival those complexities of the human body. The non-qual is also issued a submarine booklet separated into sections called blocks (sections require a signature sign-off that indicates having successful knowledge of that list of systems). Qualifying is a slow and methodical process, with a "hurry up end game." It's so time consuming. In order to keep up, learning all the facets with accuracy. It's best done on the first try. There's no time to go back to relearn. You're on the clock to fulfill this unrealistic and mandated curriculum. There's a time limit for learning submarine qualifications, two patrols for most of us. It requires constant cramming without resting the brain. Down here, the brain survives off of three things, sugar, oxygen, and sub quals.

The non-qual (not qualified in submarines) has exposure to the different levels of persuasion. The non-qual doesn't have time to be harassed by the crew. He needs to circumvent those trappings and to stay focused with studying qualifications. The crew cannot wait to pitch in and offer some help…to lead you astray. Although, some crew members were willing to help you get qualified, as they know we're all safer the more we all learn.

There is a lot of game-plotting by the crew for this ripe target. The crew will purposely play with your brain and misdirect you. If you come across as a know it all, you become entertainment. They will hand you some extraneous bullshit, then send you on your way. Calling ahead, they hand you off to someone on the other end of the boat. You are then intercepted several times during your four hundred foot-plus trek to the other end of the boat. The non-qual will be sent on several scavenger hunts to find, touch, and to locate items that really exist, and others that do not exist. He will spend valuable time, days in some cases, being bounced around by the crew. He will learn port from starboard, bow to stern, overhead to below decks, including all the stuff within those parameters. The non-qual will enable himself to find the needle in a haystack, through the confusion, by separating fact from fiction and all that he has been told. The non-qual will learn about and separate the phony baloneys from the authentic mentors on the crew and he matures a bit and gets tougher through the process. Eventually he will find the "go to guy," with the real scoop on that section of the boat. Finding key people in order to attain their knowledge is the answer to a successful learning approach. Remember, this could be a separate course in itself. There are approximately 140 crew members onboard to intercept you. They all can be nice guys or as many pains in the ass. If you need to get signed off by them, you're at their mercy. Just shut up, be nice, ask, and learn.

Allying with other trusted non-quals, and taking direction from other crew members, maybe a wiser method to the process of elimination. Sorting out who's who could be tricky. It's time consuming a must for the non-qual who has only valued time and none to waste. Standing and learning his watch station, doing ancillary required assignments, studying quals, eating, and resting, a non-qual's time is consumed and swamped with this list. The crew will stay on your case if they catch you at a movie, sleeping or while delinquent getting behind in quals. You must keep current with your quals. No rest for the weary. I took a short nap hiding in plain sight near the torpedo skid, they missed looking there. Resting on ten pound bags of onions and boxes of garbage weights was another spot in the torpedo room, uncomfortable but horizontal. It worked. It was my secret hiding place. When the scouts were looking for me, the torpedo men didn't give me up. Sleeping on the commode was another good spot. This was a spot that was easily overlooked. I turned the game back on them. It was my free time and I made better use of it.

Making adjustments in dealing with the different situations during sub quals takes some creativity. They were keeping tabs on me even though I wasn't dink, (delinquent). I needed the rest. I had to catch 40 winks to fuel up, in order to mentally and physically survive. Capturing a few extra winks was a rare nap situation. When you are that spent, you can sleep standing on your head. This was a game beyond hide and seek. For me it turned into a game of hide and sleep. I gave anyone looking for me the slip. Find me if you can. " Hide in plain sight was my mantra." Leave me alone. I can manage my own time. I've earned my time off, which included a scarce, but short nap. The need for me to remedy the situation was the replenishment of guaranteed energy. A quick nap was recharging my internal battery. Find me when I'm awake was all I asked. A rested sailor is an alert and safer sailor. Exhaustion is dangerous on a sub.

Time management of sub quals is a physical endeavor which is stressful, and exhausting. It strips away your mental energy which leaves you running on vapor reserves. The non-qual cannot afford wasting time revisiting any missed parts of sub quals. Taking enough time is critical in trying to remember facts about many systems. Brain system overload leads to guesswork while moving forward. This is often risky with big time setbacks by forgetting critical parts of systems. Repeated steps eat up valuable time. Sub quals are all about time management. There is no time to develop study groups as no one is on the same page of the learning curve. Grouping together to study is tough or impossible. There are too many interfering schedules. Almost no one is on the same exact place in the curriculum as you. Partnering up with a hidden mentor (a rare find) who is old school and qualified is the best case scenario. This is achieved by an accidental situation rather than a sought out effort. Accidentally stumbling across a big brother can be most advantageous and lucky. All learning of this nature becomes a face to face experience. But, it was something you couldn't depend on. Limited information can be passed on to you as a one-time event. Get ready or you'll miss out. This was the era before modern communications. With this in mind, learning was risky, scarce, and indeed, a slow process. Mentorship was nearly non-existent, but sought out by those aware of the need and able to make opportunities happen.

A WORD ABOUT SUB QUALS
(SUBMARINE QUALIFICATIONS) ~

Each patrol there are always a handful of new non-quals checking aboard. The non-quals are an assortment of enlisted men and officers. Getting qualified is a requirement no matter where you're from, and regardless of your rank. Without the distinction of earning and wearing the "Submarine Dolphins" on your chest, you can't be in the submarine service. The time needed for qualifying is normally one patrol for officers, and two patrols for enlisted men. The officers are schooled in submarines extensively before reporting aboard, so they can easily finish qualifying in one patrol. They have already studied concepts and functions of systems and equipment. They have the edge in qualifying. They luckily escape the time consuming harassment and bullshit that all of the enlisted men go through. Sub quals are stretched out for two patrols for enlisted men. Each patrol is 65-70 days, including sea trials. It is a daunting experience, filled with many complexities, intricacies, and thousands of facts which will test your learning capacity to the max. It is an intimidating task of dealing with the qualified crew who will help you on your qualifying journey. The non-qual will run into the department heads when they are in search of mapping out every square inch of the boat. It's just part of the process. There is nothing personal about it. Although sometimes, they twist it to make it appear that way. They will place road blocks in your path just to fuck with you. It depends on their mood when you show up to ask for their help. It's like some stupid agenda that takes place every patrol. Some form of God damn dumb form of entertainment for the crew. A non-qual is at times a victim of their impulsive behavior and cruelty. Bring your mood meter with you. The non-qual is kept in the dark as the true nature of the crew's intent. The crew is sending them on their "rite of passage" message, the hard way. The crew sees you as their play toy and entertainment for as long as they can prolong it. Like a cat with a ball of yarn, the non-qual has no idea of the length and degree of this unforeseen punishment. Sub quals are by nature an extension of hell week. They match all the crap in every detail of the sea trial routine, you're just pretty much on your own for the rest of the patrol. Sub quals are not a smooth ride by any means.

The qualification process continues relentlessly 24/7. You must stay on point to complete this abundance of grueling facts and bullshit tasks. Due to the lack of sleep, rest is a highly sought after commodity. Getting answers to problems with qualifications is accomplished slowly. The non-qual must sacrifice his sleeping time, replacing it with qualifying time. Asking the correct person is the key. That person needs to be willing assist you, and you need to catch him at his work station, and in the right mood. He must have plenty time to explain, and he can't be rushed. You're on his time, not yours. Most of the time, if all of these conditions are met, co-operation from him is yours. Filtering out who does what, is the time consuming process. If he is a trusted person for the other non-quals, he will most-likely be honest with you too. However, there are some among the crew who will twist the truth. They'll catch you off guard, and further stretch the game for their own entertainment. As a non-qual, you feel singled out to be picked on. You can bet on it, but not all non-quals are treated the same.

My roommate Chris said that he spent four days straight qualifying without any sleep. This put him ahead by leaps and bounds into quals. I asked for his secret? He said he brought three jars of instant "Taster's Choice" coffee. He then mixed in three heaping spoonfuls to a regular cup of coffee. This was his boosted caffeine formula for staying awake. He was "wired," before the term even existed. He must have spent many of these four day marathons during qualifying, even being harassed by the crew. Chris managed to accomplish earning his Dolphins during his first patrol. We didn't talk about sub quals living together. No one did. It was party time. I just now learned of his method of this true and amazing achievement fifty-years later, during a recent phone call.

BRAIN CRAMMING ~

This is a process of a compressed series of unknown facts, given to you to be learned at a laser-jet speed and applying a nonstop moving schedule to challenge your mental capacity. This borders on the impossible, yet it can be achieved. But, only if you are willing to sacrifice sleep. It must be accomplished during a cramped span of time, due to an onslaught of mental obligation and lack of proper rest. Your energy level reads zero, but you must press on. You are driven to a point where you want hide, to just vanish somewhere. This is a bleak and dreary outlook, but it feels real. It's easily compared to a three year intense by condensed curriculum. It's comprised of psychological studies, structural engineering, human behavior, and other ancillary-collateral spinoffs. It's shoved into a 120 day learning period of time. This is the average allowable time for learning all this stuff. I sometimes see it as a miraculous feat in learning. This is an underwater "Hellhole University." Welcome aboard to submarine qualifications (101).

This is my insightful experience to a first underwater encounter. It's living compressed, surrounded within the extreme confines of a submersible. Finding your space and fitting into this rat maze society, within an unrefined environment, is quite remarkable. Plus, it is subject to unexpected, unannounced, and unknown changes, which always lie ahead. Adaptations to these factors are difficult to say the least. It's a good thing it only happens once in a life-time, or 5 times in my case of 5 patrols. It is a submarine ride with no rushing back in time to relive the thrills or details. What makes it livable is that the 120 day window is broken up into two sixty day time periods. The agonizing part is leaving paradise in the middle of my ninety day off-period returning to finish sub quals. This is a version of "to hell and back," to re-engage another blistering period of submarine chaos. The studying process is like remembering, studying, remembering, forgetting, and re-remembering. How's that for getting your brain twisted? It's a complicated learning curve to say the least. This is a "distressful must" in remembering the sequences of sub quals and all the shit you wade through to get those precious Dolphins.

With that said, upon returning to Waikiki, my first mandate was to automatically forget sub quals. This was a good thing and a must! Time now to debrief my brain and to focus on the real world again. I'll turn off my brain and deal with the consequences later. This long awaited return trip is a must time to clear my mind so I can properly recover, retrieve and re-enter the human race. I couldn't afford to forget what it was like before, risking the chance of totally forgetting my real life experiences as I knew them. I need to keep current with the here and now. I needed to push out the past reminders of the last submarine patrol and hit the reset button to my former life. Besides, I needed more time to re-introduce myself to those "suntanned beach-beauties." I'm way behind and must catch up.

EXPLANATION PERCEPTION ~

I was a non-qual assigned to the Grant for the first time. My impression of the crew changed after my first two patrols of sub quals. I was no longer a non-qual when I earned my Dolphins during the second patrol on the Grant. My perception of the crew was in constant flux and my last three patrols were not quite as severe as the first two. I'm qualified. It makes a big difference. Nonetheless, my opinions were already imbedded. The crew's attitude towards the non-quals made it that way. They treated the non-quals with intimidation, and disrespect. Non-quals were under the silent scrutiny of criticism, treated less than human and lower than whale shit. This culture carries on forever, or until you're qualified. Earning and wearing your Dolphins set you apart. The physical boat was the same. It was the same in structure and appearance. My changing attitude of the crew influenced my perception of them. It was a constant change from one patrol to the next. Ahead, are different descriptions of those perceptions. They may seem repetitious, but you will find changes in them, covering all the changing aspects. The objective purpose of this underwater reality, is to keep an open mind. Anything down here goes, because there are no reliable patterns of behavior.

PERCEPTION ONE- A FRIENDLY VERSION ~

Life beneath the surface of the ocean aboard the Grant is a different and odd experience. I see it as an underwater moving prison for us rats in the can. We're underwater and underway, for the next sixty-five days, with no direction. You're just in motion. It's eerie and unsettling when you think about it. A time and space continuum with no final destination in mind. It replicates space travel. There is forward movement, but its nearly undetectable due to the slow speed. There's just enough slow speed to maintain depth control. Compass heading are constantly changing. The real heading is a secret to all but a few. It's all on a need to know basis.

We just keep going back and forth in a designated area that travels to nowhere and has no end. Added to this eeriness is a crew of 140 salty sailors as your shipmates. These salty sailors may or may not give you a bad time while you're here. They may look familiar, but they're all strangers. They each have weird quirks. They may or may not like you. Some of the crew is spread out so thin you see them only in the chow line or in crew's mess. Food and movies are the only morale boosting factors aboard a sub. They are the only homing beacons that bring the crew together to one spot. So, don't get in their way. These salty dogs are not here to make friends. You will soon find out about the loners. Experiences that are engaged will be unfamiliar and viewed from different perspectives. Down here you are self taught, self guided, and self schooled. I made five patrols on the Grant. Amazingly, I survived all of them successfully and returned to reality at some point. Some crew members talk about their 10th patrol. They've been around forever and they're either hardcore, or easy going professional sailors. They like their routine. They want to be left alone. They don't cause any trouble. They enjoy a good movie and packing away copious amounts of food. Quality doesn't matter too much to them. Don't mess with these guys. I was able to adjust to the new routine of doing my job. Many other assorted adjustments are made while qualifying. It's just the way things are in a totally different world. Choosing with whom to collaborate as a mentor was key to survival among the nonquals. It was just as important to steer clear of those who were up to no good. My secret of blending with the crew was to act a little different and off-centered. They seemed to like us off-beat people. I adjusted to the crew. Which, by the way, was always in flux from one patrol to the next. New crew members replacing some of the transferees made it that way.

PERCEPTION TWO - THE OTHER VERSION ~

Realities of life aboard a submarine consist of many layers of ubiquitous shades of grey. Your former world of black and white (clear and concise forms of familiarities), will disappear. They won't exist. Your attitude, habits, manners, your ways of dealing with people and other traces of normalcy of the human element, are disconnected and flushed away. The familiar characteristics of your personal being are put on hold. You're forced in abandoning your regular personality, friendliness, and your composure. They're not needed down here. Over a period of time, the crew will give you new ones. You will get a nickname and a new identity. They will dictate how they want you to be known. You will encounter and undergo subtle transformations along the way.

Consider this as a life saving ring adaptation. It's survival in the face of odd and bazaar behaviors and new realities. Nothing down here can match who you were before arriving here. You're aware of change, but you're unable to put you finger on it. Facts that are given to you are bogus. Your mind is challenged to remember who you were before. Well forget it, you won't have time to think about it. You begin by out guessing yourself. You are too busy to stop and think. Normalcies of life and routines of familiarities are gone. These are the facts. Your previous existence is camouflaged, hiding in the back of your shelved memory. Flashbacks of your old confidence are questionable or have disappeared. Relearning to learn is fuzzy. It's like your mind has been coated with something foreign as a misty haze. Your mind is tweaked by the ambushers of your thoughts (spread throughout the boat). They're waiting in turn, to get a piece of you. Be cool, you need to get your qual sheet signed off. Your thinking is vague, unsettled, and subject to change. The added clutter is to keep you guessing and confused. There's a silent message that gets under your skin. They like it that way. Surviving is observing and sidestepping many of their hidden traps. It's Darwin's law in practice, "survival of the fittest."

The old salts with nothing else to do, enjoy overloading your mind with distorted and extraneous facts. It's an attempt to mentally cripple you. They try to slow you down and often misdirect you. You need to decide when you're being caught in a stall pattern. These are pesky, annoying, bothersome people spread throughout the boat at sign-off duty stations from bow to stern. There's no escape. As you proceed to question your new purpose in life, different concepts of reality will come into focus as you blend more with the crew. This foreign introduction to a new reality of mental transformations you will undergo, and must accept. You will pay the price if you resist. It's ok! It's only temporary, or so you tell yourself. Never accuse anyone, who is trying to help you, of giving a "wrong answer." I caught on quickly, keeping my mouth shut and not challenging anyone's advice. You can be subjected to a sudden setback. You'll have no idea from where it came; and you will be subject to a mental ass-kicking. Welcome aboard rookies. This could be considered submarine brainwashing. Some are so accomplished at their craft, they could be considered "professional experts" or (professional assholes). The ravages of paranoia and claustrophobia can strip away your inner being, if you allow it. Keep everything in perspective. An elite men's club is trying to break you. So, pay no attention and learn to bypass their cruel intentions.

PERCEPTION CONTINUUM ~

The crew continues toying with your mind (this is normal behavior for them). This is submarine qualifications (sub quals). Sub quals is more than just a check-off list. It's a process of learning and remembering. The crew is going to put you through their hellish paces, through the meat grinder. Their objective is to wear you down, to get you back on the delinquent list (dink list), to finish you off. Getting checked off on your sub quals sheet consists of many kiss-ass visits, then a few visits to filter out the correct answers of information you will need to get qualified. This is the mapped out process for you. Maneuvering through the boat and connecting with the right person who will eventually help you is a difficult undertaking. Remember, there are 140 of them to filter you through. Sub quals sometimes can be disguised as a scavenger hunt. It is time consuming and filled with surprises and frustrations. You cannot afford to lose your cool. Remember, you are still an integral member of the crew. You need to stand your watch station, clean up your areas, do you ancillary assignments, and not to forget to eat and.....sleep? Sleep is a luxury. There is not much of it. You're aways up and running as a non-qual. Remember, eating is the only pleasure for morale you will get. If you're behind in quals, no movies for you.

Sometimes you will learn a few secrets from an unknown ally at the dining table. Dealing with old timers is the key. Once in a while you can ask a question, and pick their brains at the same time. Otherwise, it's a long chase to locate them while they're on duty and squeeze them to get signed off as they follow their routine. Many time they will ask you to come back to get re-quizzed. Returning is a bitch for a busy schedule and a wasted effort. There are many wasted trips during quals. There are many (thousand) of pieces of info you need to learn, master, apply and remember. The faster you learn the information, the less you are likely to forget what you just learned. Prepare yourself for filling up that empty brain of yours. It's like today, finding your car keys in the refrigerator. (It's ok, if you're planning to drive your refrigerator to work). A cognitive mishap of forgetfulness, when did this happen? Keep your brain engaged during sub quals. It makes for a smoother ride.

During the qualifying process the non-qual will use a trial and error method. He will soon realize that he needs to filter out the phonies from the informed crew members during his studies. They will eventually gain your trust in giving you reliable information and the straight dope. Weaving through this process and getting ambushed at every turn can get old quickly. Persistence pays off. The non-qual gets ahead when he recognizes this is a game perpetrated on him. It may take some time. The crew is made up of some professional liars. Some work at convincing you otherwise. The non-qual has to separate in his mind, bogus information and bogus untrustworthy sources from, the real stuff. Once this is accomplished, he can move on with qualifying. He is at the mercy of the task master in getting the qual sheet checked off on every system of the boat. But, signatures are just the beginning of the endless turmoil yet to be endured. Good luck non-quals.

QUALIFYING IN TWO PATROLS ~

Sub qualifications involve more mental and stressful protocols than physical ones. This adventure continues 24/7, lasting sixty-five days at a time, consisting of two back to back patrols. However, there is a three month break in between. It is grueling, but just part of the program. It is an organized, accelerated pace of learning and retention. Your memory and focus must be close to one hundred percent. You must physically operate with little or no sleep. You are constantly battling mental fatigue, but you must stay mentally sharp at your work station. This includes performing other collateral duties outside your normal scope of chores. You find yourself in competition with other non-quals. The non-qual must forge ahead, taking it in stride, absorbing abuses that come his way. It means enduring the bullying process and pushing through to achieve the learning curve set forth. Your progress is being silently monitored by the crew. Other than knowing you've learned a system and got signed off, there is no positive feedback of your standing. You need to stay off the delinquent list. You are pushed and encouraged to keep up by your non-qual peers. All non-quals (except Chris) make the "dink list" during the process. Magnified interference makes it that way. Your internal drive must kick into action. That helps you on an even keel. You need some help to get off the list. The crew is taking notice of your progress or lack of it during your qualifications process. They quietly critique your work and they can inject more or less stressful obstacles to slow you down or to move you forward. If you're not liked, it's tougher. Remember to be a chameleon by blending in with the others, by joining the flow. They are testing you to the max-brink to see if you can handle the pressure that comes with the job. Do they want you as a crew member? Are you worthy enough to survive the system and evolve as a future crew member?

Sub quals is a rat race. It's not against each other, but against time. The rat race must be realized within the confines in which it occurs. After two patrols it has a must be done completion date after learning the following: all the pieces, parts, functions, procedures, percentages, measurements, capacities, numbers, locations, counts, operations of, and calculations of every machine and system on the boat. This is a small sample test for your memory skills and the tasks you'll need to exercise and store away for future use. The accuracy of your memory will be exposed and tested from now on. Learning it correctly the first time is the key. Get confirmation! It is difficult relearning something that was learned incorrectly. It's like playing the puzzle called Sudoku. One mistake affects all that follows. Searching out the beginning of the error can be a time consuming task. During sub quals, collating a list can be worse. Getting your mind back on track is a good thing. Be smart in side-stepping these problematic situation. Don't walk off with a big question looming over your head. Nail down those loose ends. You will learn to find the good and trusted men, and to stay clear of those who willing handout misinformation. Stay on point learning one system at a time by learning each thoroughly. It can be a big mistake juggling two at once. Your mind can't absorb anymore confusion than it's already subject to. At times, mentally multitasking seems impossible. It's that little problem of being attentive in a state of sleep deprivation. You're damned if you do, and screwed if you don't.

START OF PATROL ~

We set our course for deeper waters outside of Apra Harbor, Guam. Maneuvering Control (back aft) cranks up some nuclear speed. The Captain clears the bridge and takes us down to where we level off at our ordered depth. Finally, we are underway to begin our patrol. What bothered me most was not knowing where I am on the face of the earth. These are pre GPS days. Everything was plotted at the navigation (nav) table. The navigation table was affixed to the Control Room floor. No one was allowed to stand and stare at the nav table with the exceptions of the quartermaster, the navigator, and the officers. It was strictly a "need to know basis." Well, I wasn't allowed to look, but I still needed to know where I was on the map. I got caught staring at the nav table a few times, but I couldn't make out where we were anyway. There were too many lines and fathom markers on the map interfering with the true identities of any discernible features. Although, I could still remember how to find myself in the dark. By grabbing my ass with both hands, I knew where I was on the face of the earth. With a large handful of comfort, I knew I wasn't completely lost.

DAILY LIFE ABOARD ~

When first checking aboard, the crew must adjust to the boat's artificial atmosphere and lighting throughout the boat. The air-conditioning keeps us cool and the ship's computers alive. Computers and other electronic equipment are spread throughout the five major compartments. They emit constant variations of humming noises that seep, filter, merge with, and infiltrates into all the spaces of the sub. Even those sounds that are muted allow for no peace and quiet anywhere, as they can penetrate to find you sleeping. The cool ambient temperature of 60 degrees is mainly for preventing the equipment from overheating. The submarine acts as a refrigerator. Cold ocean water transfers its cold temperature to the steel hull. Being in an encapsulated atmosphere makes it that way. The cold atmosphere promoted longer sleep patterns for the crew. The crew, instead of being subject to normal sleeping patterns, are in more of a state of hibernation. The hard work during their shift and cooler ambient temperatures effected deep sleeping. Qualified sub sailors get a lot of rack time at sea. It's a simple routine once you're qualified. You eat, sleep and stand watch. During the off hours there is poker, cribbage, bridge, table games, ship's library, coffee, and cleaning up yourself after a long hibernation. The evening movie commences every night. Regular surprise emergency drills interfere with sleeping and other daily activities. All hands must stop what their doing and participate in saving the boat. NOTHING ELSE MATTERS! We are as one.

The ship's activities committee announces sign-ups. During the patrol there are a few (smokers) boxing matches held in the aft end of the dining hall. It's a way of settling differences with gloves and headgear. It's entertainment for the off duty crew to watch. The radio shack prints up a daily newspaper of usually one sheet. Other calendar events are posted, such as contests of: bridge, cribbage, chess, checkers, poker and even cockroach races. The daily menu is posted outside crews Mess. Need your laundry washed? Bag it, tag it and hand it over to the designated Laundry Queen. Shipboard life can sometimes get boring, although the crazies aboard keep you stimulated. Non-quals have their own agendas and are kept busy studying their qualification. Heated arguments among crew members can rise out of nowhere. With the exception of smokers, fighting between crew members is not allowed. Another way of handling problems and differences of opinions was the creation of the "Bitch Log." The Bitch Log is an unofficial approach to problem solving outside of navy regulations.

The Activities Committee hosts smokers, usually on the patrol, allowing the guys to challenge each other and to let off a little steam. Into the patrol, teams race their cockroaches down makeshift cardboard alleys. Twice a patrol, the walk-in freezer gets defrosted. The whole crew gives a hand unloading. They hold off showing the movie until it's done, two hours later. The freezer is reloaded to match the menu. There's no digging around to find the next meal. We eat our way in with the next meal that sits behind the freezer door. Ninety percent of frozen food is meat, 10% other. Fresh foods such as vegetables, cold cuts, and miscellaneous items are stored in the walk-in fridge, port side across from the freezer. Our cooks bake bread and other flour based treats. Ten pound bags of fresh onions and hundreds of 50# bags of potatoes, along with the garbage weights, are stored in the Torpedo Room. These items serve as ship's ballast. The mess cooks activities include removing deck plates to find and fetch food stuffs. Thirty-five pound square silver cans of flour, pancake mix, biscuit mix, salt, pepper, sugar and coffee are stored everywhere under the steel deck plates throughout the boat's decking. Even though the deck plates are metal square grates, seeing through them is not a problem. However, it is a guessing game for the mess-cooks to fetch the bulky cans as all are shiny silver cans. It takes a 16" screwdriver with a 1" flat blade to unscrew each of the deck plates. There are 6 screws per plate to contend with. Many hallways throughout the boat are equipped with steel deck plates. The majority of the under deck stowage is in the Missile Compartment. There is enough clearance to crawl beneath the grate to get to the cans. The cans are a bit randomly tossed into these areas when loaded into the spaces. The contents of labeling is marked only on one side of the can (good time for a nap). Articulating the heavy cans can take hours. Finding the correct can that is being sought out, and hauling those out one at a time to the galley eats up a lot of valuable time. The duty cook usually chews your ass for taking too long. The big #10 cans of vegetables are stored in a locker forward and port side of TDU room. The TDU room (trash disposal unit room) is opposite the walk-in refrigerator. While in port tied to the sub tender, trash is taken across the gangway and disposed into the dumpsters. When at sea, shooting trash to sea is the recommended method. Actually, the only method as we never surface to do the job.

THE BEGINNING OF SUBMARINE QUALIFICATION ~

Sub quals is a comprehensive and intense learning process which is most often finished in two patrols. The (qual sheet) qualification sheet is the submarine's outline of curriculum, which is carried by the non-qual to gather signatures (the sign-off process) after studying each sections' system thoroughly. This is demonstrating your knowledge while getting an oral quiz on the spot by a senior person at his workstation. If he's satisfied, he can sign you off. Sub quals is broken down into submarine systems which are in the same related field. It is represented by multiple pages contained within each section to be studied and learned. Several systems are separated into blocks. All systems must be discussed, diagrammed, memorized, and physically touched if possible, before being signed-off by the division officer (who may or may not give you a sketchy oral exam). Other qualified personnel who work in the sections of the boat, performing their duty or watch areas, contribute to your learning process. Like the human body broken down into systems and functions, a submarine and its components and functions mirror that of the human body. It is just as complex and as intense a subject, or both, when studied in detail. By the time you're done with sub quals, you are a "self contained compendium of submersibles." You may not think of or know anything else as your brain too crammed beyond the full limit with all that information. It is lengthy, detailed, time-consuming, a back breaking-study, and independent of any other kind. The "brain bashing" encounters when learning makes it that way.

FIRST BLOCK ON THE QUAL SHEET ~

To illustrate the basic components without giving away too much detail is the first block of sub quals. The section on tanks and compartments is by far the easiest system of all. It can be learned in one or two days. It will take many more days, in your spare time to review. You must place them on the sub in your mind and remember. The truth to be told, there is no spare time. Sometimes a Diving Chief (usually Jordan) would put the helm in "auto pilot" and say "study quals." You will learn the equipment in every compartment, along with every hydraulic, electrical, and waterline that runs through it, plus all the valves associated with each for emergency isolation purposes. There are approximately one hundred and fifty tanks on our class of subs. These tanks are either hard or soft, (exposed to sea pressure or not) with locations scattered throughout the boat. All items that make up the sub's structure, internal components of machinery, valves, gauges, and indicators, must be learned. Also, all the damage control kits in each compartment need finding. The non-qual must be able to identify them all. Walk up to it, and place his hand on it. This indicates that he knows exactly where it is located. Other knowledgeable descriptions must be addressed and memorized. These include: names, locations, functions, capacities, color, kind, shape, contents, how many, where, when, and why. You need to discuss the backup systems for all emergencies and in detail. Fires are another big threat on subs. You'll need to know the locations of 75 pre-connected fire hoses that are spread throughout the boat, along with 150 fire extinguishers. Flooding is another nemesis that can occur. Where are the hundreds of damage control stations and the damage control kits located? What are in the kits? What do you do if the item fails or disappears? Where do you go next, and to do what? All emergencies have area leaders (heads), but all must know how to fix a problem. These are all valid questions that will come up during the six hour oral examination ending the last stage of submarine qualifications.

Initially, there is a written exam which can last several hours. The process is followed by a walk-through with your division officer. Then, finally you'll be hammered with questions for five to six hours. It's a brutal session by an oral board made up from a mix of enlisted men and officers. There are no others. Procedures and a memory test of thousands of facts will be covered during this qualifications inquiry board. They will dig deep into your knowledge for details you should possess. It is paramount, given the life or death situations that will rest on your shoulders as a future crew member, that you be ready to do what is needed in any emergency. This is very serious stuff. This is why the non-qual must develop good organizational skills. Note taking, diagramming and asking a lot of questions to the correct people, are important aspects. Organization and reviewing are key to cementing all these facts in your memory. Reaching your goal as a non-qual while being smothered in the world of fatigue and confusion is quite a feat. Mapping out your progress on a calendar keeps you on track. This is comforting in letting you know where you stand with what you have learned and what lies ahead. The finish line is somewhere out there. At some point, you must back track and review all systems with attained signatures, before moving on to the next block of sub quals. Then, somehow, you need to tie them together to make sense. The process is easier said than done. Each system and block gives you a better integrated picture of the whole wondrous machine as a complete functioning submarine.

Learning about submarines, their functions, systems, and their complexities, I realize that the characterization and nomenclature closely parallel those of the physical makeup of the human body. Below is a list of some of those comparisons of submarine systems and the systems of the human body.

PHYSICAL LIKENESS ~

There are many systems with-in the human bodies (HBs). Likewise, submarines (SUBs) have many systems one that mirror the human body. HBs have a brain. SUBs have computers. HBs have blood and both arteries and veins. SUBs have hydraulic fluid, both main and vital hydraulics. HBs extract oxygen from the air. SUBs make air from water. HBs have skin and bones. SUBs have steel plates and steel frames. HBs have internal organs. SUBs have internal machinery. HBs have eyes and ears. SUBs have periscopes, radio, radar, and sonar. HBs have heart energy. SUBs have nuclear propulsion and diesel power. HBs have an excretory system. SUBs have diesel exhaust, filters, and TDU. HBs have kidneys for filtering. SUBs have sanitary tanks which are pumped and blown to sea. HBs have leukocytes to ward off any infections. SUBs have weapon systems to ward off any invaders. HBs are human. SUBs are human, 140 strong, to function properly so as to do our jobs. SUBs are a special breed, occasionally classified as SUBHUMAN. This is a good thing. Both HBs and SUBs each have their own purpose in life. Today, HBs have cell phones. Yesterday SUBs were the first Android prototypes. SUBs have a sense of direction and they make their own potable water. HBs are hidden among the billions. SUBs are hidden under the seas and oceans. HBs produce methane gas which leads to pressure on the system. SUBs discharges hydrogen gas overboard, while making oxygen with O2 generators. Sometimes HBs when releasing methane gas, can be heard. SUBs when releasing hydrogen gas, could cause to be heard as an explosion, destroying machinery that can kill crew members.

ROUND TWO OF SUB QUALS ~

Returning to sea for another punishing round of sub quals is expected to be worse than the first. Information from the first half of sub quals must be retained and reviewed for a later date. However, new information from the second half of sub quals, yet to be learned, is stacked in combination with the first, quite a learning feat under any circumstances. Somehow, both are squeezed into the second half of sub quals, which are subject to a thorough comprehensive testing process by the end of patrol. Passing a three step testing process for the final examination meets the requirements for submarine qualifications.

Returning from paradise and jumping back into this learning quandary is an untimely reversal of events, which doesn't include a warm up period. Was I ready to tackle the dreaded second half of sub quals? Once again, I was mentally gearing up to totally immerse myself into this studying-profile-bubble. What else was I thinking? What did I forget during my time off? Most likely, everything. When we left Guam to start our break, I made it a point to forget and debrief everything I'd just learned. This was a risk I was willing to take. The freedom in front of me was too alluring. It was necessary to clear my mind and prepare for some serious Rest, Relaxation, and Recovery. Needing to vacate my mind required a clean slate for re-entering the world of normalcy. It required some "roomier mental space." Now that I'm back, I need to refresh my memory of all that was easily lost, but not totally forgotten.

Getting back with the program, I seek some self motivating inspiration. Yet, action is what's now required. Finding that learning groove again to mentally transition from leaving paradise and return into this underwater sub-culture can be difficult. Running down systems, running down answers, and running down signatures is my future outlook. This sub run is more demanding. The past few months off was merely a flash in the pan. And I'm still recovering from the adversity of the last patrol. The welcome back-mat doesn't seem very friendly.

FINISHING UP QUALS- THE WRITTEN EXAMINATION ~

The second half of sub quals requires twice the effort and memory, simply due to recollection of the first patrol systems. They all need to be brought to the forefront of your memory once again, as you will be tested after you painstakingly fill out and complete your qual sheet. Procedures are followed a perform all qualifications on submarines. The end is in sight. Reviewing all the data learned during the two patrols, you are ready to start the three parts of testing. The results of all three phases are scored pass or fail.

The first part of the test is a written exam. This part is to test your submarine knowledge in its entirety. There are approximately 7 questions that requires complete and thorough answering. The scope of answering for instance, one question would require 6-8 pages of paper. You are given a legal size pad of lined paper and 3 pencils with which to write the answers. The written portion of this test, as I recall, lasted approximately four hours. I remember writing as fast as I could in fear of forgetting the answers before they hit the paper. I sustained writers cramp during the test. The answers are hand written. I took breaks several times, which are allowed. There wasn't any time limit, nor anyone hovering over you, although the test monitor was somewhere close by. I was the only one testing that day and my division officer was the exam monitor. A few days later, it was announced that I'd passed the written portion of qualifications.

Next, in the qualification process, is the grueling and lengthy walk-through portion of the exam. Again, this was with my division officer. If I recall correctly, this was strung out over three days, involving several hours each day. He was very methodical asking his questions. My answers needed to be just as methodical in matching with his questions. This required no casual type of answering. Responses needed to be spot-on. There was no rushing. A great deal of effort with instant recall was spent in order to get through the walk-through exam. Remember, there are several compartments with several decks to each compartment, containing many pieces of equipment, machinery, tanks, lines, valves, and other objects and things to trip you up. The walk-through involved all of these decks with all their various components. Any of several hundred of questions can be created as you move through the boat. Pointing, explaining, and answering will be the theme of the day.

THE WALK THROUGH EXAMINATION ~

This is a sample of just the beginning of a walk through: My division officer and I are strolling through a compartment. We would suddenly stop and he would point at something, and ask what is that? You would give him the correct answer. Then he would follow with, what is that valve there? What is in that hydraulic line there and point to it? Then he would say, without turning around what's the name of the tank behind us? What's in it? What is the capacity? Is it a hard tank or a soft tank? Then he would ask, what is in the forward compartment of this one, and port side of the thermal expansion valve, down low, what is it? What color is it? Where is the nearest fire extinguisher. What kind is it? Where are the emergency phones (1MCs) to the Conn, to the Captains quarters, and the Engineering space? Then another volley of questions follow. Questions such as: You discover a minor leak/ flood in the middle level of that compartment. Where do you find to call on the nearest 1 MC? Then, what would you do? You go down one deck and two compartments aft, name the five tanks in here, name them as you touch them. What is the purpose of that valve? What happens if it breaks. Where does that hydraulic line end forward? Literally touching is confirmation that you know what you're explaining. Reach up, bend over, crawl and find, is part of the touching routine. It seems like after 300 touches, you're done.

This question and answer period mirrors a mental scavenger hunt. He will continue asking questions even more ridiculous than the one before. All in an attempt to trip you up. Even this portion of testing is called a walk-through. We can be standing at one end of the boat, and pull questions from the other end, and without physically being there on site. Questioning can get outrageously creative. Such as, here we are in the torpedo room. From here, tell me about the main machinery parts in machinery space #1? What about machinery space #2? How about the second deck of the missile compartment? He can pass you or ask you to review further and return tomorrow to finish.

Anything can happen. A walk-through is complicated and stressful. It is not as hectic as the oral board, which is the next and final phase of testing. Good luck to me. It's time for a bathroom break.

THE ORAL EXAMINATION ~

The day has arrived and it's brought to your attention that you passed the walk through portion of the testing process. Your Division Officer has signed you off. Now the next phase of submarine qualifications. It's the final stage, and the most important. It's the dreaded Oral Board Examination. At this point the non-qual is still in cramming mode. He is cramming. Reviewing to cover everything he has learned over the past two patrols. He is retrieving information from his written notes, and from mental notes seared into his memory of steel. He needs to re-think what he has forgotten during the off-period in Hawaii, an easy going, forgetful time. It's time for getting swept up by a period of wine, women, and song. During that three month period of total leisure, our minds have turned into putty as a result of being away from sub quals, including the relentless cramming mode that comes with it.

As a look-back, in hind-sight, I could care less about remembering the valves on the emergency ballast blow systems on the sub. My focus is swept off to my paradise retreat. Which to me means, twisting the valves on my sweetheart who is standing in front of me. This is the most anticipated moment in a sailor's life of debriefing. The R&R period is a time where all that hard laborious learning is put on hold, lost and maybe washed down the tubes. Paying the price of forgetting could come back to bite you in the rear during the oral board. Too much of a good thing is still good, yet a major ass biting in retrospect, can be regrettable. Drawing a blank during the oral board is bad news. To keep current, reviewing your studies during the off period is a good thing. Who would have known? Balancing risks and rewards with resulting pleasures, regrets, and consequences can be burdensome to your mind, and when it's all behind you, it's a fantastic relief. You're soon to be a member of the "elusive submarine fraternity."

Time passes as the qualification board assembles. Crew members are selected to participate on the oral board. They convene among themselves to select and review, who's asking what (How are they going to stick it to the candidate). In all fairness, it will be a likely overview of the submarine broken down into sections in its entirety. Each section or (block) will be discussed by the board participant whose specialty is that section of the boat. Ripping into details can reveal the non-qual's knowledge, or lack there of, during discussions. Questions relating to the submarine's functioning and emergencies will be key in all the questioning.

The oral examination is conducted at the officer's board room table. This adds a little formality to the testing process. It's the largest table on the boat. An overwhelming feeling of nervousness follows you into the boardroom. You're by yourself, facing many. You're standing at the behest of the firing squad and suddenly realize that you are the weakest link in the room. There is no one standing behind you to whisper the answer in your ear, should you draw a blank. Your ass is on the line. There is a panel of 6 to 8 participating crew members that sit on the oral board. It is an uneasy setting. You notice some panel members, you can barely remember seeing them since the beginning of patrol.

The panel is made up of a volunteer selection of enlisted men and officers represented at your oral board examination. This includes your division officer. Each member represents a specialized section of the boat. Most are heads in their departments and will usually give a good blend of questions. The oral board exam can last up to six hours, straight through. It's over when they're completely satisfied. It is a grueling test opening the back doors to your hidden memory banks of stored information, and then to release and get it all out. The non-qual answers to the best of his ability. Results of the exam are again, pass-fail, with no holding back or in-between. Those who pass are announced days later in the morning bulletin. An informal surprise celebration is held later for them.

After each patrol, when our crew was relieved by the oncoming crew, there was a traditional gathering of the enlisted crew to celebrate the giveaway of the Dolphins awards held at Andy's Hut. There was a big turnout. This was the only social event held by the crew after surfacing. The two patrol non-quals were now deemed qualified in submarines. They have earned their Certificates of Achievement and their Submarine Dolphins. However, it is not completed without the final act, which is steeped in tradition. In my group there were five of us.

There was a large gathering of the crew at Andy's Hut. We were each treated to a mystery alcoholic laced beverage with ingredients selected by the crew. We stood watching as these liquid cocktails were built for us and to be consumed by us. Crew members would haphazardly select 8-10 shots of the nastiest liquor choices available. The liquors were collected in the bartender's mixing can. It was topped off with all the various beverages and mixes! Included and not to be neglected, a swirl of green Creme De Menthe, floating on top. This lethal concoction is shaken for proper blending, then your Dolphins are dropped and allowed it to sink to the bottom. The idea is catching the Dolphins with your teeth while chugging this reprehensible and deadly drink. The experience resembles a refined method of water-boarding. If anyone could die from alcoholic poisoning, it would be here. You have now received your Dolphins. Be sure to have a "good-heave before you leave" Andy's Hut. It is a colorful conclusion to the submarine tradition. Praying to the stool gods actually marks the final act of the submarine experience. What a proud moment to behold, yet necessary to avoid feeling like "death warmed over" the following morning.

I now earned my Dolphins. It has been a exasperating long-haul for earning them. Now, I can now rest easy and relax for a spell. I've earned that quiet time. And, sooner than I expected, it was suggested by some division chiefs that I should enroll into an "A" school. After reviewing the schools to choose from, I really didn't have one in mind. Torpedo man, Sonar man, Radio man, Quartermaster, et cetera, none of these choices appealed to me. Before choosing, there were other issues that needed to be addressed.

The "A" school choices were in San Diego and not available when we were at sea. The schools were only available during my off-period. No way was I going to school right after a grueling patrol! I needed some serious R&R time on the beach in Waikiki. I had just scored a great place near the beach and I needed to spend some vital time there. "A" school would be an interference to my plan. Besides, after finishing "A" school, there would be no guarantee that I would return to the Grant and Hawaii. I couldn't risk the chance of not returning to the Grant by going away to school. I needed to be in Waikiki during the off period to gain a better foothold in enjoying local events, and to lay the ground work for a future career. I planned on staying here after my navy time expired. Also, "A" school offered little training to bring to the table after discharge. And, I wasn't planning on shipping over as a lifetime sub sailor. The raise in pay wasn't that great of an incentive to sign up for "A" school. Plus, I was half way though my four year obligation. I set my goal on getting out, so the 120 day early-out was a welcoming and attractive incentive.

After "A" school, the incentive increase in pay wasn't enough to sway me into signing up. Leaving, just when I'd returned from sea, wasn't going to happen at any cost. I viewed "A" school for those sailors who wanted to ship over after a 4 year hitch and to receive bonus pay. I decided long ago, after my four years ended, I was a goner. Time passed and we were at an impasse for deciding school or not. I finally got the word and the issue of choosing was abandoned. Being pigeonholed into a career choice didn't set well with me. I didn't mind. School meant getting uprooted and reassigned to a San Diego school that was only available during my off-period, a conflicting of time for when I needed to enjoy myself. Attending school during my off-time was a definite "No." And, it was my only consideration. That is, attending school in San Diego only while the Grant was at sea. This was the main underlying issue. The non-flexible school schedule would be cutting into my plans. So I passed on the whole idea of school. I valued my own time-off and wanted to savor it at my own pace. I needed to relax, veg out for awhile. The thought of attending another school during this time was an irritating and quickly fading thought. I needed to cultivate room for establishing residency here, after the end of the navy. I had reached my fill of studying. Also, I didn't have a naval career in mind.

Instead of choosing an "A" school vocational training, my duty on the sub was a dedicated Planesman, along with doing other collateral duties such as part time BCP Operator, Auxiliaryman Forward, etcetera. A deal was struck with the Interior Communication section. So, my role became a person in training with a planned curriculum attached to the IC (interior communications) gang. I was under the tutelage of IC Supervisor, Caudill. He took me under his wing. I studied "A" school courses aboard the sub. I was biding my time. I'm too short on time to plan a naval career of any sort. Meanwhile, I focused on enjoying my off-time just as the other crew members.

THE PLANESMAN ~

The Planesman is the driver of the submarine. His job is to keep the boat at ordered depth and course. He also controls the "bubble" or the levelness (the attitude) of the submarine. Bubbles are marked in degrees up or down. The skills required to do the job are like flying an underwater, slow moving aircraft. My reality was jockeying a steel beast through the underwater highways of the ocean. Keeping it on course and at ordered depth requires reading dials and gauges, and adjusting to them. The slow speed of the boat is a hinderance in controlling a sub of this large size of 420' long. Operating the fairwater planes (as in any other job lasting many hours at a work station) leads to proficiency. Mastering the planes is an art-form which allows for better anticipation to counteract any articulation of the sub's movement through any sea condition, depth, speed, and course changes. I actually became one of the very best at it. Rumors (scuttle-butt) was that I was number one at that station.

There is the use of a steering wheel on a post that moves in and out to assist you. The servo valves in the post makes a squeaky noise as the hydraulic fluid surges in and out. Unlike looking out the windows of the airplane, a submarine has no windows, you fly blind. The Grant crawls through the ocean at a purposely slow speed. It's truly "silent running" of the mission. There is a lack of forward movement at this speed. However, there are detectable movements in shallower depths caused by the ocean surface action. My job as the planesman, was sitting at the inboard station working the fairwater planes. There are two of them, attached one on each side of the boat's sail. The two planes are little wings that articulate up or down through the use of an attached center hinge. The other station located next to mine is referred to "the outboard station." It controls the stern planes and rudder. It adds necessary controls to the submarine's movements. The majority of the time, the submarines' operating controls are set up using Automatic Maneuvering Control (AMC). This feature is equivalent to today's operation of driverless cars. However, any ordered changes of the boat's operating attitude must be switched back to "hands on, control," using the talents of the Planesmen piloting the inboard and outboard stations with their professional touch. There is also a setting where one Planesman can operate all three articulations, using the fairwater planes, stern planes, and rudder, if necessary.

Maneuver this approximate 8500 ton behemoth, up and down to keep the proper ordered depth and course is kind of fun but not at all easy. Driving a submarine requires constant concentration, focus, anticipation and reaction. Experience at the controls is priceless. In comparison to driving a car, well, there isn't any. Driving a car, and when you lose control, you can aim for something cheap. If control is lost, the worst you can do is to broach the boat (accidentally pop out of the surface). This is unacceptable, but sometimes unavoidable. Keeping the boat hidden (the stealth) is the main purpose, but chances are slim that anyone is looking anyway. The vessel's required slow speed is constant, therefore, it is difficult to articulate the boats' drifting ups and downs. When the boat is at periscope depth, (shallower depth) or in rough seas, the surface action of the ocean has a natural tendency to suck the boat to the surface. The physical dynamics and interplay between the long flat missile deck and that of the surface action of the ocean allows this to occur. The interplay between these two forces gives your skills a intense workout while preventing broaching the boat (making holes in the ocean). This would be compared to correcting a car while in a skid, but not oversteering. But the anticipated movements in a submarine are those related to the constant up and down fluctuations, while fighting the surface reaction. They come several times per minute. If the planesman loses his concentration, the sub could be sucked up to the surface. This could be compared to one of today's video games. It's keeping everything on track and within the limits of perfect suspension, and doing it blindfolded. It is a constant fight between the sea and the Planesman keeping the ordered depth. The effort in keeping control is more extreme in heavier seas. While watching the depth gauge, the reading of the gauge oscillates between either side of where you need to be. The average oscillations, coasting between the two readings, could be interpreted as the true depth. The longer in the seat as a Planesman, the better you get with the experience. The more miles you log, the better you become. At this point, mastering driving a sub, could be considered an art form. I personally logged tens of thousands of miles as Planesman in the underwater abyss; but not to know physically where I was on the face of the earth. Even to this day, it's bothersome and haunting.

The "floating wire," as we call it (the boat's antenna) trails behind the boat on or near the surface. This is our vital communication link to the outside and must be in place 24/7. It is also susceptible to being cut by the boat's propeller in wild seas and when the boat is at the wrong downward angle. As mentioned before, broaching the boat is another unexpected bad maneuver which is always possible. This occurs when the top of the boat (the sail) unintentionally breaks the surface of the water. Our mission depends on the stealth of invisibility, a vital concern when controlling the boat.

My claim to fame, according to others in the Control Room, was that I was the master of controlling the boat in rough seas, especially at periscope depth. It was noted that my job accomplished this with precision. I didn't realize I got such high praise. Unbeknownst to me, and due to my hidden talent, I was assigned to the helm during battle stations. During my time behind the steering wheel, I kept track of the number of floating wires that I cut during my time on the planes. The four wires I cut in the past, were obviously overlooked (just part of the learning process). My assessment, as I remembered, was purely cutting two wires by accident in uncontrollable seas. The other two wires, were inspired by nudging the edge of the envelope. It was simply a silent test of my accuracy. The whole experience of controlling the steel beast was equivalent to riding a multi-thousand ton wild bull at an underwater rodeo. I'm sure that there were some undocumented cases of sleeping bodies in berthing that came close to being shaken out of the rack when the boat was brought up in turbulent seas. Seat belts for sleepers would have been a handy suggestion, but not practical.

There were the functions of the fairwater planes, the stern planes, and the rudder. These three mechanisms kept the boat on a true heading (course) and proper depth. There were two seats manned with Planesmen (one port, one starboard) to operate these three functions. The diving chief was located at the six o'clock position in between these two stations. Verbal orders were given to the Planesmen. He also barked orders to the ballast control panel operator (BCP). All depth and course orders came from the officer of the deck (OD) or conning officer. He was the duty officer at the time, and had control of the boat. Co-ordination in using these available assets made for a good ride.

There was also a duty navigator to plot the courses of our physical locations and to advise the (OD) of his updates. This was the basic makeup of the Control Room, the nerve center of the submarine. The (OD's) his toys, such as the periscope; and each shift, the (OD) always had to flex his muscles by operating the periscope. Any and all major sub function orders were controlled from there. To increase or decrease speed, just call (engineering space of the sub) maneuvering to dial up some nuclear propulsion. The majority of the time the boat was in (AMC) automatic maneuvering control speed. Sensors for keeping the boat on course and ordered depth worked great. The ballast control panel operator (BCP operator) monitored and maintained the trim of the boat by pumping water from one tank to another, flooding water in, also pumping in or blowing water out. The BCP aids in the boat's diving, surfacing, and trim levels. There was a navigation table located here with an assigned navigator. This was our GPS system back then (plotting courses on a map).

Outside of the Control Room is the sonar room, the eyes and ears of the submarine. From the radio shack (radio room), where we received outside radio traffic and top level action assignments. The Radio Shack created a small newspaper each morning from captured radio traffic that float outside, throughout the airways. The newspaper was only one or two pages. A copy was posted outside crew's mess for everyone to read. Radio would get all excited when they lost the incoming signal. Sometimes in rough seas, with a runaway down bubble, (the sub gets into a sharp angle down, attempting to regain ordered depth) the propeller can cut the floating wire (the antenna). It's a key piece to our communications. Losing the signal causes panic in the control room and all hell breaks loose. The Captain is immediately informed. There is a rush to string a new wire in the sail. This has to be accomplished while the boat is in the broached position, giving away our stealthiness. Throughout the operation I can imagine the radiomen in the sail getting beat up by the boat's movements. I barely recall cutting the wires (a common occurrence) three or four times during my time at the helm.

And the boat's propeller had no mercy. The planesman job was a difficult task controlling the boat next to the surface. Both broaching the boat and cutting the floating wire were always possible, and a bit rare. The wild seas have the power to turn your submarine into a floundering, bobbing cork on the oceans' surface. It is a fight to get the sub back down and then to maintain control of it. During this short span of time, the name of the "Control Room" lost its meaning.

MAKING THE CAPTAIN'S REPORT ~

Every morning at 8am sharp, a report is made to the Captain. It is a verbal report delivered by the Planesman to the Captain in his stateroom. The stateroom is located at the far end of a passageway, just forward of the Control Room. This early report details the function of the Control Room at the start of every day. Subsequent reports update the Captain as to current status of the boat, and any changes throughout each day.

The Captain is usually seated at his desk, port side of the door. The only light in his stateroom is the desk lamp. He is often busy making entries into the ship's log. His rack is across the room, straight ahead of the door opening. The master head and additional storage are located to the starboard side of the door entry. After knocking 3 times, the Planesman hears, "enter," and steps just inside the door to give the Captain's report. The report includes the status of the boat, such as date, time, depth, course, and any pertinent information the Captain should be aware of. When the report is completed, the Captain usually says, "Thank you, that is all." The Planesman answers "Yes Sir," then steps back to leave the room and pulls the door shut the as he exits. This is the standard Captain's report procedure. I've made several of these reports during my time on the Grant.

The Captain's report one morning was somewhat unusual from the others. After knocking, I entered his stateroom. The door was still open behind me. The room was completely dark with only the hallway light shining into the room. The Captain obviously overslept. He was still in his rack as I started giving the report. I could feel the boat rising to periscope depth in heavy seas. The boat was tossing side to side. The door behind me slammed shut with a loud bang! I was startled, caught standing in total darkness, thrown off-balance by the rocking from toe to heel, heel to toe. Suddenly, I was launched off my feet and flung forward. I stutter-stepped to break my sudden forward movement, my arms locked straight out to keep from hitting the bulkhead across the room. I fell downward, short of the wall. I heard a loud startled yell from the Captain when my left hand and arm crashed into his upper thigh while my other arm landed on his lower leg. I realized what occurred when I fell forward. He turned on his bunk light. I composed myself standing by his bedside and finished giving the Captain's report. Then, I turned and immediately exited the room. Somehow, he forgot the part, to say "Thank you, that is all."

ALL ABOUT COCKROACHES ~

Cockroaches come in all sizes, big, small and in between. Their size is no indicator of their speed. Some of the larger ones, 2 1/2" or bigger are sometimes lethargic. It all boils down to their genetic makeup, as in all of living things. They're crunchy when you step on them; and most usually die when lying on their backs, legs straight up. They have wings under their tough exterior shell, although they don't fly often. I observed the roaches on many evening strolls along the Ala Wai Canal, located just a half block from the cottage. Avoid bringing your date to the canal for a moonlight stroll. It will cause too much needless excitement, and a good stiff drink will be needed after the walk.

There are thousands of cockroaches breeding by the canal. I learned to spot the fastest ones. They're good for racing on the boat while at sea. Cockroach racing was allowed in the sub. It's one of our elected past times. It's accepted and classified as harmless entertainment. Once the patrol begins, the races are scheduled and posted.

Fun, excitement, and betting are great for the spirit in looking forward to something to pass the time. Prior to the race, cockroaches are logged-in, and gathered up for training. These pesky critters sneak aboard hiding in the corrugated cardboard boxes brought in with our food supplies. Teams of three are registered and representing their roaches. The roaches have dinky painted numbers on their backs for easy identification. It takes a steady hand for painting the IDs. Four foot long racing lanes are constructed from the cardboard boxes available in the galley. Six lanes across with lane dividers, raceways are constructed with short 2" tall walls to contain the critters. Many cockroach heats are run with a process of elimination to determine the winner. Money changes hands during all the racing heats. Betting money definitely adds to the excitement.

Danny, the Chief Commissary-man who is head of the galley, has an extermination method for the roaches and a process to head-off any future infestations in the galley. The cardboard food boxes end up in the galley to be opened. Tearing apart the cardboard seems to activate the dormant critters, allowing them to spread throughout the galley to find new breeding territory. Danny's self created extermination method occurs twice a patrol. The proven method is done simply by using boiling water. The lower stainless steel shelving and cabinets are emptied of all the pots, pans, and miscellaneous items. Boiling water is tossed into the empty voids, cracks, and crevasses to kill the critters, including their eggs. The stainless steel cabinets and shelving is not affected by the boiling water. Everything that ends up floating is then mopped up including roaches and their eggs. The boiling water also acts as a sanitizer, and the method doesn't take much time at all. The Goat locker could certainly benefit by looking into this sanitation method.

THE MYSTERIOUS CHASE ~

I have heard that submarine sailors are selected as candidates, based on their high test scores, related to their intelligence. After volunteering for the Silent Service, their next assignment was entering submarine school. After submarine school, they are assigned to submarine duty, or various "A" or "B" schools, depending on their chosen interests. It all seems a simple enough process. However, their true intelligence is not revealed until reporting aboard. There it will be demonstrated, in action. From what I have gathered and observed, the new non-quals reporting aboard the Grant have lost some of their intellectual prowess, including something called: common sense. I am convinced their common sense was overlooked by not getting tested. Assuming that their common sense is questionable, I can assume it is up to the crew of the Grant to find out where they stand. By sending them through our testing process, we will be confident of adopting worthy crew members who will save us all during an emergency.

Here's the reason why this is brought up. I once witnessed a non-qual from Texas. You know the type. One of those "know it all types with an out spoken loud mouth that rambles on." (I have nothing against Texans, he just happen to be from there). This one showed a lot of spunk, you know bragging and such. He also stated that he knew about everything, including all there is to know about women. He shared his sexual exploits of them. So, we the crew saw an opportunity for him to get his common sense tested. An impromptu and made up test was used to find out if any common sense existed at all in the "Texan."

We sent him on a mission, to search for, and to locate, a used "Fallopian Tube." Thinking it was a vital industrial part of the submarine's equipment, he was excited about starting his search immediately. The crew surreptitiously gave him the run-around for two days as he went searching for it. "And for some reason, he couldn't find the damn thing." His search patterns included several trips, from the torpedo room back to the engine room. This is a distance in excess of 400 feet apart, with several deck levels and compartments to navigate through. Back and forth he went. (A hidden mileage counter would have been fun to have attached to his shoes). During his search, he made several embarrassing inquiries of several crew members, who further added some stress to his search by telling him, with a straight face, that if he couldn't accomplish this first easy task in sub-quals, he would flunk out of subs. So he became more desperate in his search, continuing to make several more trips back and forth, begging many other crew members for help, (who by the way, did a great job concealing their laughter). After more than enough time had passed to find it, another non-qual was assigned to help the Texan. The two-man search party came up empty-handed at the end of the day. They of course, got their asses chewed for failing the mission. The crew, tired of seeing them show up at their work station, finally gave in, admitting they were made victims of a snipe hunt, and that there was no such submarine part. (The Texan was caught not knowing the nomenclature of the female). Very bothersome to the crew.

During another session of hide and seek a new non-qual, was asked to find a left handed OHM wrench. (There is no such thing. OHM is a measurement of electrical resistance). He failed in his attempt. A few days later, the same "Fallopian Tube hunter" was handed a telephone receiver only used from "ship to shore phone calls." He answered submerged 95 feet plus and underway. They told him it was a call from his mother. This poor guy, one of these "intellectual sailors," never made the cut. The boat's selection committee released the Texan upon return from sea trials. After weighing in the evidence, lack of common sense was curtains for him. Another non-qual was conned into standing by the rear escape hatch to snag the mail buoy when we surfaced. It was another ruse set up by the crew. After five hours of delays, and running short of excuses regarding the missed rendezvous, and the boat never surfacing, he got smart and called it quits. He was smarter than we thought. He was relentless at his qualifying in that he accomplished qualifying in just one patrol. That's an outstanding accomplishment for a newly enlisted, non-qual sailor.

THE BITCH LOG ~

The Bitch Log is an unofficial approach, or informal way of dealing with disgruntled crew members who need to vent their anger and frustrations somewhere. Possible resolutions and solutions are voted on by the Bitch Committee. In order to shorten the work load of the Bitch Committee, the bitch must be voted on as an authentic bitch. Many are stamped "rejected." It is ironic to name something like this "The Bitch Log" when the boat is devoid of them. It just seems strange. However, the "bitching men" loaded with complaints, make up for it. The Captain and the officers were not involved in the process. It was developed by the crew, for the crew. Bitches in the log may be posted as follows: An argument which has no end, a long going feud over some extraneous bullshit, deep seated arguments between crew members that could lead to fighting (fighting is only allowed at smokers), the crew's disagreement with operating policy, or any other matters that cannot be resolved by just bitching. The Bitch Log was created by the Bitch Committee. So, if you have a bitch, write it down. It is a stopgap for feuding crew or disgruntled members to iron out their problems before they blow up.

The way the system works is when a bitch is raised, it is entered into the log by the complainer as a new bitch. All entries are reviewed. The Bitch Committee meets and determines whether the "bitch" has enough merit to be resolved. If not, the matter is dropped. The Bitch Committee makes its recommendations to resolve the remaining bitches. If the complaints are too serious, beyond the scope of the Bitch Committee, it's handed up to the next level, the senior staff. The majority of the complaints logged by the Bitch Committee are mostly trivial ones. Some of the more serious complaints that were mitigated were based on the increasing number of lousy meals prepared by Hiyako. Another hot spot that was addressed was too many untimely drills by the officers disrupting the morale of the entire boat. The Bitch committee recommends settling grudge differences between two parties by entering them into a weekend "Smoker" (a boxing match). They can pound sense into each other to settle their differences and also have a method to release their frustrations. There are usually five or more boxing matches for Saturday evenings. Smokers draw a big crowd, fun for all. Grudge matches between officers and enlisted men were not allowed, although, it would be interesting watching them pound the shit out of each other, or some sense into one another.

SHOOTING TRASH ~

During the course of a patrol, a submarine generates a lot of trash. It's fed to the ocean everyday. The TDU (trash disposal unit) room is an interesting place designed just for that purpose. It is amazing what comes through the TDU room. As the saying goes, "everything ends up in the trash." There's no exception here. We shoot tons of trash, junk, and garbage each patrol. Whatever shows up in the TDU room, must go down. It ends up on the bottom of the Pacific Ocean. Besides the wet and dry garbage from the galley, all trash from all areas of the boat ends up in the TDU room. Other telling evidence shows up to be crushed and discarded. Bourbon, brandy, and assorted whiskey bottles are some of the unmentionable items. These liquors mix well in our paper cups. Nickel cokes were dispensed from the coke machine. There are quite a few boozers hidden aboard the boat. Today they're known as closet drinkers. I didn't know who they were, nor did I really care. Maybe, this is how they coped with their problems. In truth, I never saw an open bottle anywhere. How the empty bottles end up in the TDU room is a mystery. The sound of popping glass bottles says it all. It was rumored that wine was made from the grape juice concentrate we had on board. I met an old timer who liked being at sea for months as it kept him dried out and away from the sauce. I met another, self-proclaimed alcoholic. He didn't mind making the wine to perfect his recipe, from one patrol to the next. He was a truly talented person in his own right. He must have been Julio Gallo.

While at sea, getting trash off the boat (shooting trash) is an art form all in itself. Generally, shooting trash is done after the evening meal is served. If the galley is overwhelmed, filled trash cans sitting around and the same for TDU room, the TDU will be operational. Trash comes from everywhere on the boat. The galley produces wet garbage, including cardboard boxes and cans that need compacting. The engineering spaces from back aft produce trash of metal scraps and parts, old tools, nuts and bolts, etc. Shredded papers from the Radio Shack and other items considered junk, make it over to the TDU Room. The trash that we generate is shot to sea submarine style. The Trash Disposal Unit (TDU) is a vertical, 12 inch diameter cylinder, a stainless steel hull penetration. It extends waist high from the TDU room through the bottom exterior of the boat. The loading end of this vertical cannon (resembles a cannon but does not function as one) is where 7-10 rolled cans of trash are loaded. They are loaded one on top of the other, until the TDU unit is filled to capacity. Each can is approximately 30" tall and porous. There are two / two pound garbage weights within each can. They are inserted, before the ends of the cans are sealed shut. The garbage weights ensure the can will sink to the bottom of the ocean. The breech door is shut and locked, as in loading a cannon.

The mess-cook wears a head set, and communicates with the BCP operator who is stationed in the Control Room. It's a two man team to shoot trash. After loading, and the TDU is shut and locked, the hydraulic outer door is opened from the BCP (ballast control panel). Ten thousand gallons of sea water is pumped through the TDU, flushing the garbage out to sea. The process is repeated. Inside the TDU room is a trash compactor. It crushes everything using 1500 psi of hydraulic pressure. Dry trash is compacted within the rolled cans. The compactor-ram is a round plate (a steel disk) that compacts the rolled can from the standing end position. Wet garbage from the galley is lifted from a nylon knit bag, then placed into rolled cans, weighted, then loaded to the TDU. It makes you realize, there's a lot of trash resting on the bottom of the Pacific Ocean. Garbage resting on the bottom eliminates the possibility of a floating bread trail for the enemy to follow. Covering your tracks is elementary in maintaining invisibility. The careful handling of "shooting garbage" is just another subject illustrating how the taxpayer's money is wisely spent.

THE TRIM PARTY ~

It always occurs each patrol. Some of the crew will contribute a little stress to the new officers reporting aboard the Grant while they're making their first appearance at the Conn (Top dog in the Control Room). The crew, in order to break up boredom and stir up the morale (the shit stirrers), will organize a secret trim party. It is initiation time for those fledgling officers straight out the academy, and who had never stepped foot aboard our home, the submarine.

It is time for the crew to test their "know it all attitudes." Trim is the fulcrum point (center of balance) that is controlled by and is influenced by the ups and downs and side to side attitude of the boat. Trim of the boat is inconstant flux, never fixed for any length of time. Submarines, big as they are, are subject to trim changes. Messing with the trim of the boat requires adding or subtracting to the balance point. It also adds to the teeter-totter affect or to the side to side listing (tilting) to make an adjustment. These virgin-top-dogs need to reveal their vanity with exactness and precision. Making a good impression on everyone in the crew in the Control Room is their objective. When they notice the trim needs adjusting or they need to apply their input to tweak it in order to fix it. It will be their unconstrained participation in achieving their own failure. They have no idea.

Meanwhile, it is determined by the crew, this new-bee from Annapolis needs his attitude adjusted first and before he messes with the attitude of the boat, which he knows nothing about. He thinks he does, but the shit stirrers on board will prove him dead- wrong. He will be whacked by a good old-fashion trim party something done to ambush his confidence and to bring out the best of his immaturity in panic mode. When they're finished with this guy, he'll be old and wiser hopefully. Before the shift is over, his superior attitude will be dissolved by the embarrassing lack of knowledge of submarine trim, and that he hasn't any. Unbeknownst to him, just another lesson sent by the crew, a lesson to be learned the hard way. Book learning at the Naval Academy, for what its worth, send it straight to the TDU (Trash Disposal Unit).

Imagine when things go awry, and you loose control, it must be upsetting to the virgin-top-dog. Guessing where the trim should be adjusted requires pumping water in or out of tanks, or blowing water in and out to control the ballast. As a last resort, overworking the Planesmen. The OD's guessing continues by ordering the bubble to be increased or decreased via the Diving Chief. Ordering a depth change to get a grip on control of the trim could also be added. Doing all of this while the boat is still meandering lop-sided through the water, will cause the maddened OD to rip out the last of his hair in frustration. Mission accomplished.

Mastery of this balancing-act is impossible for a new officer. His frustrations will get the best of him when he resorts to giving orders that are unreliable (guessing at best) to the Diving Chief, the BCP operator, and to the Planesmen to do their jobs properly, and hopeful some ass chewing will get the job done. It's similar to carrying a marble on a slippery tray and keeping it centered while walking. Success is unlikely.

Behind the scenes, causing upheaval and disorder to the trim, are the shit-stirrers, one of many groups, a secret gathering of ten men moving quietly with stealth to accomplish the chaos. They join in a group moving in small pairs of two in order to stay undetected until collected in one spot. Roughly, they represent one ton of weight. They move together causing the weight distribution to be off center, just enough to be noticed in the Control Room. Then, with a little lag time, repeating it many times, at many locations during the session.

The officer, ends up chasing the trim, as the trim continues to move, from one spot to another. This could be considered payback for all those unnecessary over extended drills during sea trials, just don't get caught. Imagine the sub moving through the ocean as a drunken sailor, in a cockeyed- fashion, upsetting the (OD) Officer of the Deck. A silent message is being sent by the trim party. Try adjusting this one, this one, and this one too.

The Captain always has a watchful eye on the men under his control, for rumors and gossip have a way of spreading regarding the lack of performance of his new officers. The gossip could be fact or fiction. Nevertheless, it could reflect badly on the Captain. This is a rare example of "shit rolling uphill, instead of down hill." The game is extended to those involved, or whoever he thinks are the culprits. The Captain has his secret scouts out there surveying how rumors began. He can throw some ungodly drills into the thick of things when we least expect it. He's still the boss, and has control of the boat. If the Captain strikes back, blame it on the trim party. There isn't any one to blame. For the enlisted, it's just fun and games to keep from going nuts.

WRONG PLACE FOR A BAD COOK ~

"Hiyako" (hurry up) became his nickname. That's what he yelled at the mess cooks, "to hurry up." His rank was chief cook, but I used many other colorful nicknames when I worked with this phony and fraudulent cook. How he achieved the rank of chief E-7 is still a mystery to everyone. Soon, the whole crew was calling him Hiyako. He came aboard the Grant to fill an open billet as cook. He came off a tin can, a naval destroyer, a transfer from a surface ship that has zero respect from submariners. That could even evoke some ill will from the crew.

Hiyako didn't care what any submariner thought, as he bragged about coming off a destroyer. He was a skimmer and had no business being on a submarine. The main problem was that he couldn't cook worth a damn. Providing great chow on the Grant is the boat's biggest morale booster. His arrival, stabbed the crew in the heart, by upsetting the boat's morale, and then destroying it. From the very onset, he would cook not using nor following the proven navy recipe cards. He cooked using his own disastrous methods. The crew made sure he didn't forget it. Whoever approved transfer of this idiot to our boat made a big mistake. (Someone, probably impressed with his rank of chief cook, played with a transfer which was how we ended up with him as punishment). Skimmers can't be trusted, and they are mostly hated by submariners. Normally, a cook that is this disastrous couldn't buy his way into the submarine service. The most mysterious fact that was so puzzling was how he achieved the rank of chief cook? It must have been a clerical error, or maybe those eating his food had burned-out taste buds and thought it was all good. Just a few shifts in the galley was enough that the crew couldn't trust his meals, and it was determined best by the crew to have p&j sandwiches as back-up food when he was cooking. He was headed for a long walk on a short pier.

Remember, officers eat the same prepared meals as the regular crew. One patrol of eating this less than palatable food was enough suffering for the crew. This is definitely messing with the crew's morale. He needed to be immediately transferred off the boat. The question should be asked, how did this non-qualified cook sneak through then navy's checks and balances system and end up on our sub? Many times he served ruined food to the crew. Big mistake. One time the spaghetti dinner was so salty, the crew ended up eating peanut butter and jelly sandwiches. He got away with "serving chicken shit instead of chicken salad," once too many times. The crew ended up throwing their plates in the scullery, shouting "nice try." Hiyako was labeled the chief belly robber of the Grant. He was caught in a tough place, as his vanity was stronger than his "uselessness" and everyone wanted him off the boat. To speed things up, they even participated in filling out transfer requests for him and forged his signature. Hiyako quickly learned that his "fraudulent reputation" (unbeknownst to him) was quickly sinking him into "the abyss." Then, by continually preparing all those inedible meals for the crew to eat on a daily basis, he was doomed to return to a surface existence. Go poison them for awhile, not us. Food is our sunshine.

The last "stunt of his idiocy" (and the straw that broke the camel's back) on the list of snafus he had up his sleeve, Hiyako was caught mixing red lead paint in the galley's 60 qt. Mix Master. Hiyako, a chief cook who should have known that "lead is deadly" if ingested, and being void of any common sense, took it upon himself to surprise everybody by painting the galley floor with red lead paint. Everyone jumped his case when they learned of the incident. He got ham-strung for such a flagrant violation of naval regulations. The crew's health was placed at risk due to his bad judgement. He could have poisoned us all, due to his lack of common sense and extra dose of idiocy. Everybody on board heard about this incident and rode his ass pretty hard for the remainder of the patrol. I caught wind that the crew had to figure a way to ditch him and send him back to destroyers from which he came. Perhaps the Navy was running out of places to hide this imposter. Hiyako was lucky he didn't take a ride out the torpedo tube instead, or maybe get flushed out the TDU, as shark snacks.

Hiyako was delinquent in sub qualifications upon coming aboard. But, he could care less about getting qualified. He lacked the ability to grasp the concept of submarine qualifications anyway and somehow slipped through the cracks of being vetted for his lack of cooking knowledge and other intellectual prowess. Maybe his low score didn't set off alarms and flashing red lights, but I believe the Navy purposely ditched him by hiding him on the Grant. It was our turn, now we're stuck with him. There was a time when I was the mess cook working under Hiyako. Working with him didn't go well for either one of us. I kept myself busy just trying to stay out of his way.

Peeling at least the one hundred pounds of potatoes was part of the every morning schedule. Learning mistakes from the past, I knew peeling spuds using a paring knife takes forever. I brought my own potato peeler to save time. I saved a half an hour, or more, peeling spuds. Flying through the hundred pounds of spuds, I purposely created a break for myself, finishing ahead of schedule. However, my plan backfired when Hiyako made me cook for him using the time saved. This created an opportunity for him to use my break time by purposely steal my time off. Prior to the evening dinner service, two trays of rolls accidentally went up in flames. He forgot about the rolls in the oven. Black smoke was seen by the crew pouring out from the galley. The fire alarm sounded, and there was a full scale fire response to the galley. A report of a "galley fire" sounded and the boat went to snorkeling depth to evacuate the smoke. Dinner service was delayed and the crew was pissed by the incident which caused the delay. Hiyako was blamed for the entire mishap. The whole incident could have been avoided if Hiyako would have stood guard over the oven during his thirty minute break. Words of wisdom say: When something is stolen, even something seemingly unimportant as thirty minutes, it can come back to bite you in the ass. Could be Karma evening the score....chief?

The Captain wondered what the hell happened. There was an investigation into the cause of the fire. Hiyako was left standing in knee deep poop again. Other plans of retribution by the crew were being developed to apply some finishing touches on Hiyako. We wanted to send a message to transfer him off our boat. He knew that he was out of his element. Stubbornly, his ego was in denial. He was silently threatened by the crew, mostly behind his back. One day an opportunity became available for the crew to personally get some retribution.

He certainly had a lot of nerve stealing my time. Who was this tenderfoot chief cook anyway? He exposed by his lack of cooking talent, that there wasn't any future for him on subs. He should've stayed on destroyers learning to cook. He was a skimmer through and through. How did he ever get assigned to subs? We had a fine tradition of cooking on board the Grant, and he destroyed it. He must have been a last minute transfer. He has ruined our fine outstanding record. But after this incident, an opportunity came up so I could forgive Hiyako and his blunders. You have to remember that he was way behind studying submarine qualifications and he never was putting any effort in it. In his haste, he desperately asked me to help him with sub quals. He was warned to get off the delinquent list. He was worried, hard pressed, and seemed to be mentally scattered by this threat looming over him. He desperately needed to be shown some main hydraulics in the lower level ops. Well, everyone knew there weren't any main hydraulics in that section of the sub; but I had to pretend there were some important main hydraulic functioning in the Snake Pit. When we get down there, I would add some further stress by making him read and memorize all the tank gauges before showing him any main hydraulics.

So a plan was set-up involving a few crew members. I coaxed Hiyako into viewing the main hydraulics in the Snake Pit, to help him with his sub quals. He was nervous about the Snake Pit. Just the sound of the words "Snake Pit" put him on the verge of nervousness. Hiyako was a hillbilly from the South and probably thought there were real snakes in the "Snake Pit." (I was very familiar with the Snake Pit. It was my collateral work area as forward auxiliaryman, and I'd been in the Pit at least seventy-five times). I was certainly happy to show him main hydraulics in the Snake Pit. Other crew members listened in, as the plot thickened. The crew couldn't wait. They were grinning ear to ear and rubbing their hands together with anticipatory happiness. They were looking forward to leveling the score with this belly robber, meal wrecker, food saboteur. Gleefully they anticipated his nearing "Heave Ho"!

ENTER THE SNAKE PIT ~

The Snake Pit (SP) is an area in the boat's bilge. This is a disgusting place at the very bottom of the boat. Located in this man-made cave are tanks, petcocks, valves, and smelly sea water. Added to the mix the smell of diesel fuel and the sloshing noises of liquid lying beneath the plank and you have a fine soup. A trap door (a removable hatch) leads you down a ladder into this dark, wet, and dank atmosphere. It seals the only opening into the Pit, as if it were keeping things from escaping. It is a place where bats would live, if there were any. Describing the Pit in this manner added to Hiyako's fear of entering the Pit. It is a nasty place with barely enough room to turn around to take readings from the gauges. It is a fulcrum point of the boat and it's hard keeping your balance. There is a slight side to side sway standing there. The Snake Pit is the location of Sanitary tank # One, and Sanitary tank # Two. Sanitary One is where all the boat's toilets empty. Periodically, someone goes inside the tank to scrape the sides. How was he chosen for the job? Dumb luck! This tank is blown to sea when full and is emptied. (Today's environmentalist get upset about oil slicks. Are the subs to blame?) Sanitary # Two collects all the grey water from the sinks throughout the boat. This includes galley water, water from the sinks and the shower drains. This tank is pumped to sea when full. When this was explained to Hiyako, he became completely confused and lost.

The Snake Pit is located below lower level ops in a passageway to the port side head. There is a large oval shaped wood gridded hatch covered with plexiglass that is situated in the middle of the floor. It is just outside the port head and weighs about ten pounds. It is a tight fit squeezing your body through the only opening to access the Snake Pit. There is a short 6' ladder into the pit and there is a secret light switch location next to the ladder. It's attached behind it and should be turned on before going down, because it is pitch dark. And it only lights one small lightbulb. The light is insufficient for illuminating the entire Snake Pit. There is a six foot plank by one foot spanning the center of the floor. It's orientated port and starboard, and very narrow. This is where you stand to record the readings and turn valves if needed. Do not lose your balance and step off the plank. (There is a shallow but nasty drop off that awaits you). Looking aft are the walls of the two potable water tanks. We make our own water and it is sent forward from back aft where it is produced. One tank is always being filled and is vented. The other is servicing the boat's water needs and is pressurized. (Just guessing, maybe 40 pounds of pressure). When the one tank runs out, it is switched to the tank which is full or being filled. The now empty tank needs to be vented to receive potable water. This procedure is done by turning the valve as fast you can for venting the once pressurized tank. It vents, with a loud deafening screeching noise into the Snake Pit. (If it is sudden and unexpected, you might consider changing your shorts from the scare. It lasts about twenty-seconds, enough time to quickly empty all your orifices). The two valves for venting and pressurizing are next to each other. Switching over the tanks can be done with one maneuver using both hands. If done smoothly, the boat will not lose any potable water pressure. The day before showing Hiyako the nonexistent main hydraulics in the Snake Pit that "he requested" to learn, I explained and covered all the important steps he needed to know before entering the "Pit." It was my opportunity to add some worry and trepidation to Hiyako's concerns regarding his upcoming adventure. I purposely neglected to tell him to bring an extra pair of shorts.

THE SNAKE PIT BITES HIYAKO ~

It was time for Hiyako to enter the Snake Pit. I got there earlier to turn the light on so he couldn't find the location of the switch. I waited for him to arrive. We uncovered the hatch together and climbed down the access opening. He was lost and confused as he fumbled with his notebook and pencil. This buffoon was totally overwhelmed by all the valves and piping down there. I started pointing to different areas of importance, each more important than the next. I was making up confusing explanations of it all. I did this purposely and rapidly to overcome his listening and comprehension abilities. (I even got lost in my own confusing explanations.) He listened, eyes wide open with an accompanying blank stare on his face. Remember, the area was dimly lit as I directed him in the corner down low to the farthest point in the dark. "Bend over and look low. Around the corner there are some main hydraulics," I said. "See it," as I pointed to the dark corner. Because it was dark, he couldn't see anything. Steadying his balance, he got down lower for a closer look. I reached down and opened the vent. Deafening and screaming air shot into the Snake Pit. He fell to his knees from the shock. I scampered out, flipping the light switch off, leaving him in the dark. Someone quickly set the hatch cover over the hole and stood on it. All we heard was Hiyako yelling obscenities through the venting noise, beating on the underside of the hatch and threatening to kill us all. The thing is, with his cooking he could.

When it was over, nothing was mentioned about the incident. Hiyako kept his mouth shut. He was too embarrassed, I suppose. I hope this incident sent a message that he is out of his league as a cook, especially on this boat. I believe it finally got through. It's too bad such extreme measures were used to get a point across. His recklessness performance in the galley, along with his bullheaded attitude, was to blame. It was the best way to handle the situation. Hiyako didn't waste any time putting in a transfer back to destroyers at the end of the patrol. He was finished. The skimmer had had enough. The experience in the Snake Pit ended his fledging submarine cooking career. I realized the event was a "mean caper," but with good results, and for the health of the crew. He had put me (and the crew) through a lot of hell for the past several months working under or with him. It was redemption for me; and justice for the greater good of the crew. Lighting a fire under this stubborn cook was a last resort. The incident in the "Snake Pit" finally broke Hiyakos' stubborn attitude, which helped to expedite his self-imposed, and crew urged, transfer off the boat. Hiyako can use his experimental cooking skills somewhere else. It seemed as though he never possessed any "submarine common sense" and reached his "peter principle" long ago. Regardless of his circumstances, down here on the Grant he was definitely a cooked goose, and at the perfect temperature of "well-done," finally finished!

A REPLACEMENT COOK ~

Another "cooking wonder" who showed up on our boat was Skip McDuff. He was another cook who thought he could impress the crew with his cooking talents in the galley. Unlike Hiyako, this one got qualified in subs, and he showed up as a transfer off another boat. Nevertheless, he still had to qualify on the Grant. It's the rules. Unfortunately, during my rotation, I worked as his mess cook. He was a cook who's food was barely edible. McDuff quickly gained for the galley the reputation of the "Shit Shack" when he had the cooking duty. He was bossy and abusive with his authority. By using us mess cooks, he was able to cover his fuck-ups and failures. His galley was in constant disarray and messy as hell every duty shift he served. We had to keep up with all of his messes, then cleanup after him. He was slow and showed up late several times for work. He was warned about his tardiness. His food quality sucked and his ability to follow orders was his weakest point. His talents,… none existed. He had just arrived and complaints poured in from the crew. He was, because of quals, always in a big rush. McDuff was always in a state of panic to get the food out on time. Tasteless garbage was served up more times than not. He would alter the proven navy recipe cards instead of following them. The crew could tell who had the duty in the galley, judging from the amount of scraps left on the plates. They would pass in line tossing their plates into the scullery, yelling: "nice try McShit," including other disparaging innuendos. Danny and John Lemieux (McDuff's bosses') were always micromanaging him in the galley to oversee the quality of his food, keeping the crew from going ballistic. The bosses were finally obligated to square him away just to prevent a mutiny aboard the Grant. The "squaring away" never fully succeeded. He was simply too much of a lazy and quarrelsome bastard. The crew wouldn't put up with another Hiyako and was only just barely better.

McDuff was jealous of Lemieux's cooking talent, ever since Frenchy's return from CIA chef school. He attempted to emulate

John's creativity. John was given free reign with recipe experimentation, and in doing so, his meals were always beyond excellent. McDuff, without any approval from his bosses, followed in Lemieux's footsteps in taking liberties in redesigning his food. His attempts, led to lots uneaten food tossed in the garbage, which led to his eventual reputation as "Shit Chef." Many times the crew resorted to eating peanut butter and jelly sandwiches to make up for the lost meal.

Following sea trials, McDuff was warned against going ashore to get drunk at Andy's Hut, but he went anyway, blowing off the warning. The next morning McDuff was stuck (for punishment) in the galley as duty cook under the watchful eye of John Lemieux. I showed up as the mess-cook, and for the upcoming entertainment. I witnessed McDuff weaving and carrying his puke pot around, barfing up strands of green slime. The boat was at periscope depth and weaving everywhere was McDuff. He was begging to be relieved. McDuff was sea sick and still drunk from the night before. He was suffering a well-deserved double whammy. John said, "you should have heeded my warning." He was ordered to finish his shift. Then I jumped in to finish him off. "Hey Mac, a fried frog covered in whipped cream would be tasty right about now." Mc Duff responded by heaving up the last of his stomach contents into the six quart pot he was carrying around just under his chin. Following that, he had the dry heaves every two minutes. I worked for McDuff for weeks as his mess cook and I wanted to send him a little "fair's fair" for the petty and the needless shit he put me through. After all of his failures as a cook, McDuffs' mind was still in "la-la land." He continued thinking that he was a notable chef onboard the Grant.

The truth of the matter, he would be lucky to qualify as a lousy fry cook at a "dumpster diner." His shoddy meals swamped his delusions of grandeur. He was a zero asset in the galley and the crew knew it. My illusion, was that he needed an "emergency ride out the torpedo tube." The crew agreed with my thinking that a little mock mutiny would be in short order. Let's load him up! I was ready to push the button! But first, let's duct tape that pot over his head as a finishing touch. Even the sea turtles would get a laugh, as he whizzes by.

THE JUNIOR GRADE LIEUTENANT ~

Life in a submarine can be a relaxed atmosphere between the officers and enlisted personnel. We all get along better in a casual atmosphere which is easier to function in. It's always better without the yes sir, no sir, dramatic protocols. However, the new Lieutenant J.G. who reported aboard the Grant should've known better. As a matter of fact, this was his first time of reporting aboard anything. He brought his arrogance aboard heaped atop his superior officer attitude. One day he unwittingly unveiled it to me. My philosophy was not to mess with, nor piss anyone off. This is the code by which I live. I've found it much simpler to operate this way, especially around sensitive sub sailors. Sometimes walking on eggshells is required. In the case of this junior grade lieutenant officer (Mr. JG), he suddenly stopped me when passing me en route to the Torpedo Room. He just had to chew my ass for as trivial a thing as not calling him "Sir" in my morning greeting of "good morning." He vented on me. I assumed he wanted to exercise his authority by lecturing me about protocol. But I realized he just needed to impress me and feed his J.G. ego. His worldly way of charming me wasn't working at all. I could tell he was struck with a superiority complex since he'd graduated from Annapolis; and he couldn't wait to use it on someone. I hope to return the favor soon. This was his first tour on the Grant or any sub. It should have been quite obvious that such formalities were not used down here. Officers or enlisted men, down here we're all equals. I soon realized that we had a failure to communicate. He was lecturing me about showing respect to officers. Staring at him, I was thinking who was this (just out of the academy) all star? Before we parted he gave me a stern warning to call him "Sir" next time we met. Prior to meeting Mr. JG, I had no problem with the other officers of the Grant (minus Mr. Happy). I seemed to have a smooth rapport with them.

Mr. JG seemed to be suffering from a lack of respect as a naval officer. Why was he acting in such as strange manner? Maybe his wife cut him off before going to sea? I thought that Mr. Happy and this J.G. could start their own club, having that in common. I could have been mistaken. Maybe, he was lately separated from his wife probably "for her not calling him Sir" prior to having sex. Whatever the case may be, my conclusion was that he possessed rookie traits, straight from the academy. No one clued him in on how to interact with crew mates on a sub. Obviously, he was unaware his first job was to qualify on the Grant. His other job was to meet and get to know the crew members, including me. I pulled more weight on the boat. Being qualified, I garnered more respect from the crew. I was a trusted crew member. He had much to learn and I wasn't going to show him the ropes, unless he scrapped that attitude. He had already set a questionable tone with the crew. As we parted, he still had a chip on his shoulder about not being addressed as "sir." He has much to learn about a slight twist to human nature. I should have demonstrated some sense of humor by snapping to attention with chest out, and throwing him a salute. Maybe, that would have met with his approval, as long as I didn't laugh.

Subconsciously, I chose Mr. JG as my next patrol project in teaching him a lesson in humility. We'll see if he can eat a little crow for being such a nincompoop. He needed to demonstrate a better attitude with strangers. Down here, not only did he step aboard the Grant but he entered the dimmer side of reality. He needed to ditch this superior officer attitude of his former life. We have our decorum too, that he needs to recognize, and respect. Until he adjusts to the new world, he can stick his protocols where the "sun doesn't shine." Down here, things are different. Mr. JG doesn't know this yet. Officers aren't much trusted by the crew too much anyway; and this is another example of why. I lied about not messing with anyone. He has made a liar out of me, so now I must mess with his head. I have the entire patrol to think about it. You need to know who you're dealing with. In the eyes of this officer, I was just another enlisted grunt. I will need to draft some help from my friend, the Laundry Queen, for a little payback. Mr. JG will need to scratch away his decorum, and his secret gift from me. But, this will help him get over his identity crisis. It's all just part of quals on a submarine including the snobs.

A SPECIAL TOUCH ~

Mr. JG needs to observe and learn, by slowly warming up to his unexpected future. His issues with me in the hallway was totally unnecessary. He needn't have wasted my time by over-lecturing me, just to make his point. He probably thought I would also snap to attention and salute him. Nevertheless, his lesson that wasn't covered in his "Bootcamp for Officers," is due, and forthcoming. Mr. JG will receive a little welcome aboard gift. It will sneak up on him; and he has no idea such a thing can even occur. I rendezvoused with my friend Gary, the duty (Laundry Queen), about sending him the gift. He suggested that he would take over from there.

During the patrol, he will intercept JG's laundry so he can add his special touch to the wash ingredients, which included changing the wash cycles of the washers. I was curious and I asked him what was it? Gary proceeded telling me. His secret was to handle this officer's clothing with tender loving care. His skivvies will be especially handled with a double helping of raunchy laundry soap, very little rinse, with a hard and thorough drying. Then, work out the stiffness of the material by hand. This was his proven recipe for introducing some, "discomfort and itching," the kind you can't get rid of. It's a formula which has you checking yourself for having crabs. I agreed, "that sounds great." I thanked him for his talented suggestion. He grinned at me as I left the room. He had that deviant haywire expression written across his face. I knew what was coming, had to be good.

It was noted, as a point of interest, that Mr. JG should have left his attitude ashore and created collaborators to help him mesh with submarine behavior. I realized he was immature and had a clumsy approach with people. Meeting me by happenstance was one example. He rubbed others the wrong way. During the patrol he could have approached me with questions to help him through the understanding process. I was willing to help him. All the crew members are a compendium of knowledge, individually, or as a group. We know what goes on and the different pecking orders. Despite his being an officer, he needed to wise up. We understand the crew. A rookie like Mr. JG has to learn to navigate and adapt while tapping into to this abundant source of information. Doing it smoothly, like a chameleon, and using finesse is helpful. Displaying an attitude, pushing your way in or being in a hurry, becomes counter productive. Rumors about him have a way of spreading. Hopefully, may they be good ones. Good luck, Mr. JG. This motley appearing crew is more sophisticated than you think. We hope your survival skills are in order. In a week or so, he'll be paying a visit to the doctor about his skin disorder. (If we were really ruthless, we could have sent his wife a family-gram warning her about his crab infested body). But, we're almost civilized human beings and not quite that cutthroat.

MR. SKIPPY ~

At the beginning of each patrol, the crew gathers outside of crews berthing. The (COB), Chief of the Boat issues everyone 2-4 white fuzzy cotton t-shirts to be worn under their (poopie suits) pooppee suits. The t-shirts are soft to the touch. The poopie suit, with its strange name, is a rayon-cotton blend, one piece jump suit. It comes with a velcro front closure, starting from the front of the neck to below the belly button, and it's royal-navy blue in color. Across your chest is your name tag, and on the opposite side are your Dolphins.

The strange thing about these t-shirts, even after many washings, they still shed their (lint) fuzz. Early into the patrol, when everything seems to settle down, activity of the crew slows down. Boredom starts to set in and along comes (Clancy), Mr. Skippy. He inherited this name because of the empty Skippy Peanut Butter jar that he carries with him. This is the time when he makes his appearance. You're minding your own business, and suddenly from out of no where, like a stalker, appears Mr. Skippy. He holds out his empty jar, with the lid off, and asks if you have anything to contribute, (that is, any bellybutton lint to contribute). Strange as it may seem, everyone who is confronted, reaches into their bellybutton and puts a dab into the jar. When I first saw the jar, it was half full. At the end of the patrol, the Skippy's jar was full of bellybutton lint, packed full. Many of the contributors didn't even know there was any fuzz stuck in their bellybutton, while some had much to offer.

I try to understand why Clancy does this. His action is such an oddity, you can't help thinking about it. I became aware that many of us onboard have weird quirks. First of all, I thought he was touched with a little lunacy. Was he nuts? I don't think so. He worked in the radio room. This is a highly classified area. After thinking about his strange and odd activity, I concluded he was just trying to connect with all the crew members using his own weird way. Visiting with each one of us, one by one was a hobby. His activity was definitely different but harmless. Believe it or not, everybody went along with the program and donated lint to his Skippy Peanut Butter jar. His actions on board the Grant were just considered normal submarine culture, with a little touch of odd humor anchored to it. Clancy doesn't talk during the collection. When he's done, he just zipped off, stalking someone else with his jar held out. Maybe this was a way of fending off boredom for him. Everyone liked Clancy. They play along with his amusing behavior. Maybe he does this to add to his collection of jars at home. Maybe he displays his Skippy jars on the window sill, sort-of-like patrol trophies. During my time off, I went out to Lanikai to visit my friend John Lemieux. A bunch of guys off the Grant were renting a large beach house on the other side of the island. Mr. Skippy lived there too. He was one of six roommates there.

John mentioned that Clancy possessed a habit of leaving the house in search of his car first thing every morning. Returning from his nightly boozing at the local watering hole, he would leave his car parked somewhere in the neighborhood. He would aim the car in the general direction of the house, then he would drive as far as he could, then park his car. Very seldom did he park in front of the house. Sometimes, it would be parked down the street, or sometimes several blocks away. But, no matter where he parked his car, he still stumbled his way home on foot. The first thing upon awakening, and most important to him, was to search the neighborhood to find his misplaced car. Every morning he was out on his morning hike, like exercise in disguise. What a life he led. When at home, find the car. When at sea fill the jar. It's sort of a poetic life and a busy one. Clancy was a unique character and a nice guy, in spite of his crazy obsessions.

TRAGEDY HITS THE GRANT ~

Chis Wenzl was on duty to witness the tragic event as it unfolded before him. He describes it in its entirety and relates the following excerpt in his own words:

Hawaii is the gold side of the coin; Heads. Tails side up isn't too bad either. It's real life, but only silver. Hawaii can be every possible ingredient for heaven on earth. But, for submarine sailors, there's always a price. Even if it's only a minimum of four years of your life. There are curve balls in civilian life too, but you can plan for most, short of the fender bender. Divorce was endemic in the submarine service, around 60%. You almost knew you'd find your wife just as you'd left her the last night you were together, happy. That's the slow curve you can deal with. You almost expect it, and can mentally plan for it. As in all the armed services, shit flows down hill in the U.S. Navy too. Almost most assuredly on submarines because every mans life depends on one person. And being that every man onboard is you, you don't want some weakling piece of unproven crap, who will buckle under fire. Consequently, all new "rats" get run through the mill, just to be sure they can take the pressure given them. Enlisting, physical testing, bootcamp, and submarine school, if you're there, you're a piece of excrement and you'd better knuckle under and do as your told. Be quiet, be alert and keep your wits about you. Then, you're on a sub. The U.S.S. Ulysses S. Grant was to be my first duty station.

Reynolds, 1st class (ET) Electronics Technician was a family man, 5' 9", 200 pounds and no fat. He was big at the shoulders and arms, always well groomed, clean, and had a blond crewcut. He gave me my walk-through when I first came aboard the Grant. I was familiarized with all that I had learned from schooling. He gave a compartment by compartment, deck by deck introduction to what was to become my address for the next two years (4 patrols). It was fairly general, sort of a hello to my new home. What impressed me most about Reynolds he was that kind, soft-spoken and well mannered. His main job was to maintain the computers in (MCC) Missile Control Center. Educating new "Rats" was a collateral duty he did voluntarily. Reynolds was good at it and he treated me humanely. I found it unusual for a senior (an old salt) to treat me with respect. During quals he taught me more about his job and about computers. He was always nice to me and everyone. He was obviously intelligent and a exemplary sailor, a good role model.

It's a year later now and I'm doing my job as (LLOPS watch) lower level operations compartment watch. I'm out of the sonar shack performing my collateral duty. It's an easy job. Lower level ops is mostly berthing, bathrooms (the head), crews lounge, the library, and down the hall was MCC. That's what you can see. However, every door or cabinet allows access to a variety of damage control equipment or various systems and machines. The battery access hatch, snake pit hatch, and deck plates offering access to storage space, filled out my general responsibilities as the man on watch. You wear a night stick on a web belt so everyone knows your on the clock, working.

It's a normal watch. As I walk around, I see Reynolds headed to MCC with a cup of java. He's always good for a smile. When you're on watch, you know everything going on around you and around the boat. Obviously I knew Reynolds was on watch in MCC. I also knew Kim and Trujillo were on the planes, Jordan was diving officer, Cheatle had the BCP, and Spritzer had the (Conn) Conning Tower. The Conn is the officer's perch were the periscope is located (it's their toy). I knew all these men, and they were the best at their respective jobs. They all had their Dolphins. You can't trust some of the officers or a submariner without Dolphins, yet. Kim and Chief Jordan were the best at their respective crafts in the control room. Bruce Cheatle and Trujillo were calm, qualified and able-bodied seamen also. Most officers were rarely trusted or accepted by the crew. Officers watched as enlisted men did all the work. Mostly they were pampered and spoiled little boys and assumed they were better than all the other "Rats." We were all rat-trapped. Willie Pickle was the on duty quartermaster (route plotter). Jordan was a whole story unto himself, a man with a seventh grade education and a genius I.Q. He had a great sense of humor and though only 5' 9" and a 160 pounds, you just knew he could handle himself anywhere. I always felt best when he was on duty as diving officer.

Lt. Spritzer was a real masterpiece, seemed pretty intelligent, but not quite in the real world, a little aloof, brainwashed, and too much by the book on truly meaningless matters. After I made qualifying history in one patrol, he interviewed me. Kind of a one on one pep talk, grill session. He pressed me hard to take the offer of officer's candidate school, and be a nuclear engineer for the U.S. Navy. I told him that I really didn't want that, but thanks. He said, "Well Chris, what do you want to be when you grow up?" I told him I wanted to be a Oceanographic Microbiologist. I said to him, "What do you want to be when you grow up." He was silent and dumbfounded.

So, I'm on watch and Spritzer takes us up to periscope depth. It's a normal operation to keep us on our toes. As we make periscope depth, I can tell it's a rough sea state, 1=low, 5= high. We're at least in a 3 sea state. We're rock 'n rollin in berthing, crews lounge area, but that doesn't affect "life as normal" on a sub. Six guys whom I faced many times are at the poker table. They were playing jacks or better, 5 stud, 7 stud, or a 3 card low ball poker game. The game was dealer's choice. Across the aisle was another table where 4 were playing bridge. On the wall by the 2 man table was a small innocent, little door, measuring 1' x 1'. It provides access to the periscope well. This is the bottom where the periscope seats in the vented or down position. When the periscope is worked, there is a subdued sound of movement cause by the hydraulic oil in the pipes and equipment. It's a bad choice being at periscope depth in the "iffy weather conditions." Kim and Trujillo are doing well at keeping a slight up bubble to save the (wire) floating antenna. Cheatle was on top of the ballast maintenance, but Spritzer was obviously distracted or somewhere else. He has been playing with the fine tuning knob on the periscope. He backed it off too far and dropped it down in the periscope well. That got his attention. He told chief Jordan to have someone get the knob. Jordan told Pickles to get someone from MCC to assist him in this little snafu (situation normal, all fucked up). Pickles came down to find me. He told me to rig-for-red (you can't see red light through a periscope at night). He and Reynolds (who volunteered for duty from MCC) went over to access the periscope well to try to retrieve the knob. All's red in the crews lounge. The bidding of bridge contracts and shuffling of cards are gone. No more clatter of chips as the poker bets and antes accrue. There is a low hum of background voices, the muffled whirling of various little fans, and water or oil moving almost silently through pipes.

Pickles and Reynolds take turns with a red lens flashlight looking for the errantly dropped knob. They finally locate it. Willie Pickles is able get his head in the 1' x 1' access hole, but not his arm in too. It's not long enough. Reynolds has longer arms than Pickles. Pickles pulls his head out and Reynolds takes a swing at trying to find that 1" x 1" fine tuning knob. I can see him stretching, and he says he can barely touch it. Then not 6' from Reynolds, not 1' from the door to the periscope hydraulics room, I hear the unmistakable rush of hydraulic oil gushing through the lines that raise the periscope. It's already been raised!! In an instant I knew it was DESCENDING. (Because the periscope weighs in at 2 tons, no power is needed to lower it. Gravity does the work). One second later came the almost inhuman, ear piecing, blood curdling screaming of a 30 year old healthy man, having his massive right arm ripped off his body by a lowered periscope. The distance between the periscope and the access door is 1 inch. Not enough room for a very large arm. His screams were loud and unnerving, chilling to the marrow. Grabbing the 1-MC I yelled, "Raise the periscope." "Raise the Goddamned periscope! NOW"! (the 1-MC goes to the captains stateroom, the conning tower and engineering power spaces). In the same motion, I flipped a barrel switch just left of the 1-MC, switching from red to white light. By the time I turn to assist, 2nd class yeoman Mike Asher has already leapt the table where he had been seated at, pulled his web belt off and was using it as a tourniquet to stop the blood shooting everywhere. Other shipmates tried to keep the thumb thick shred of flesh, as close as possible, to the stump of an arm that 10 seconds prior was vibrant, and strong. Now, all but gone.

It was a gory, bloody, horrific scene. A healthy, large, well muscled man is going to leak and spurt a lot of blood in a short time. His heart raced to 150-200 beats per minute and Asher's belt likely saved Reynolds' life. But, blood was everywhere, pools of it, walls, ceiling, floor, tables, people. We had him on a stretcher and the operating table (stored in the overhead of the aft mess hall) within 5 minutes and all the morphine aboard in him within another 3-4 minutes. Reynolds arm was held on by only a thumbs worth of flesh. I saw it. The Doc severed the shred of flesh, closed the major vessels, and put the arm on ice in a bag. Reynolds was out like a light.

It took hours for a sea going tug reach us. It was hell getting Reynolds across the gangway, in the state 3-4 seas, to the tug. But, we did it successfully. whew! Everything was subdued aboard the boat. We (I was leading seaman now) cleaned up the lake of blood in mostly sad ways. Not much desire for talk, only thought and sorrow. Spritzer, the conning officer who lowered the periscope that severed Reynolds' arm, nearly went insane. He never got over it. He quit the navy, but he was done anyway. With a reputation like that, he was good as dead. I heard he attempted suicide. He failed again. Hut! Reynolds got a fake mechanical limb. The Navy gave him a good retirement and hired him as a civilian to teach classes for the navy as a "techie." What a man! Anchors aweigh me boys, we sail at the break of day. Hey, Hey, Hey!

DR. BONES ~

Like in "Star Trek," we called him "Bones." As doctors go I never had the occasion to find out, but as a shipmate, he was a fine fellow. I would often find him hanging out with "Mother" Hatch in the Torpedo room. He was usually asleep on one of the torpedoes. I found out he had Hepatitis, which wasn't known until we'd been at sea for about a month. He told the Captain he'd probably be O.K. 'til we reached port in six weeks or so. The Captain let him self medicate with whiskey for the rest of the patrol. This probably wasn't such a good idea as Hepatitis and whiskey are both rough on the liver. We don't surface under these conditions, so he dealt with the situation under the circumstances.

He survived the patrol and his wife picked him up at the airport upon our arrival in Hawaii. His pale yellow skin (jaundice from the Hepatitis) could almost pass as a sun-tan. She was making a long over due candlelight dinner while he was dying from a heart attack in the bathtub.

CHANNEL FEVER ~

This a term used when the crew can't sleep in anticipation of going home and looking forward to the end of the patrol. It's a strange but common occurrence. It seems the entire crew is awake at once. Everyone gathers in common areas to chatter. You can see faces in the crowd you totally forgot seeing two months earlier. Strangely, their names are forgotten too. Sleeping is a foregone conclusion and a rarity at this point. We're slept out, and insomnia has taken over our souls. It's arousal time for the sleeping dead. A new spirit is reborn among the masses. Sleep is overrated; and you need to stay awake. You cannot afford missing the flight home cause you slept through it! The crew is friendlier now with each other, strangers united in a common bond.

GETTING TRANSFERRED ~

During my sea time in the navy I completed five patrols on the Grant, living close to one year under the ocean. Rumors were floating about during the end of my last patrol, that the Grant was headed for the shipyards in Bremerton, Washington. Before the news broke, we were already back at Ford Island. Our crew was split up. Some of the crew went to the shipyards with the Grant. Others like me, were transferred to other boats spread throughout the submarine fleet. There was nothing official, but rumors had it the Grant was to be refitted and transformed into a Trident Submarine. This most likely involved cutting the boat in half and adding a longer missile deck. (John Holmes would have been proud.) Trident submarines are named after states and not presidents, as were the FBMs. I was transferred to the USS Permit. It was the sister ship to the USS Thresher, a fast attack class submarine that mysteriously sank in the Atlantic. I learned of my transfer at a ship's muster outside the office at FBM Headquarters. We were back at Pearl. It was the beginning of our R&R period. During this time, I was granted a 120 day early-out. The early-out issuance was common, marking a turndown in the Vietnam war. This meant I was looking forward to getting discharged from the Navy ahead of schedule. This was good news for me. I was still leasing the cottage on Seaside Avenue in Waikiki. Nothing had changed with my living arrangements with my roommates. Chris got transferred in the shuffle too. He reported to the Jackson, an FBM stationed at Ford Island. Once I received my transfer papers, I reported to the Permit. The Permit was still out at sea, so I got stuck working in the sub base barracks. The Permit's homeport was at the main sub base at Pearl, located just across the harbor from Ford Island.

I was assigned a job working in the Permits' section of the barracks, working for and assigned to the Master at Arms. He was the bossman who ran the operations of the barracks. The Master at Arms was an older, overweight-middle-aged sailor. This was his life time career. He was dressed in his work dungarees and appeared as the navy stereotypical, average Joe. He was seated at his oversized metal gray desk located in the middle of the hallway. The setting and title, probably added some importance to his self esteem and to justified his job title. His responsibility was assigning the daily work load to those under him, but more importantly handing out the paychecks each month. His job seemed simple. He never bothered us and left us alone.

This was my new fill-in job until the Permit returned from the West Pac tour. The tour (the sub assignment) lasted 4-6 months at sea. It was coming into port for only a short three day turnaround, then returned to sea. This could mean that I was going with it. I wasn't prepared for that. It took me by surprise. Going to sea on the Permit meant that I would miss my 120 day early out. Several things were stacking up against me and I hadn't even reported aboard yet. This meant I was required to "qualify" on a fast attack submarine. It was mandatory to "re-qualify," in order to serve aboard a different class of submarines. Well, I wasn't really in the mood for re-qualifying nor ready to disappear on a lengthy cruise somewhere out there in the deep blue. According to my report date, it already put me behind in sub quals, before even stepping aboard the boat. I had delinquent status without even being there. The major concern was going to sea on another Westpac tour. These can last several months. If this happened, it might cut into the "early out" discharge program. This impending dilemma needed to be brought to the attention of the (XO) executive officer of the Permit. This needed to be done pronto!

During the waiting period I was assigned to the sub barracks, as the barracks attendant. Each submarine was required to leave a crew member behind as their boat's section attendant. This assignment was basically a janitor and maintenance person under the Master at Arms in charge of the building. This was my new temporary job until the Permit returned from patrol. I was assigned with five other grunts from other boats in our fleet.

The daily work schedule included swabbing and waxing the seemingly miles of cement decks of the two story, mammoth building. This included large sections of hallways which surrounded the outer perimeter of each floor, cleaning many heads was included in the cleaning schedule. The crew members of the submarines stayed on board their boats while in port. They never slept in the barracks, but were in and out of assigned personal lockers. Most likely, there was a need for the extra storage space. The barracks, absent of sailors, seemed abandoned with zero activity. It was a peaceful work place, soothing and stress free. And with no one looking over your shoulder.

My focus now was to stay here at the base and avoid going to sea on the Permit. I reported aboard when it finally docked. I found myself the following day loading torpedoes into the forward torpedo hatch, along with the topside gang. That was an all day workout. Meanwhile, I created a plan to avoid going to sea. But I needed to run it by the XO of the Permit. He was second in command of the boat, just under the Captain.

The next morning, I tracked him down in his office aboard the boat. The door was open, so I paid him an impromptu and a very important visit. My short future remaining in the navy depended on the outcome of this meeting. The XO was seated as his desk with a cup of coffee in one hand and a pen in the other going over some paperwork. I entered his office, introduced myself, and promptly said I was a transfer off the Grant. I also explained I was already delinquent in quals, even before reporting to the Permit. I included that I earned my Dolphins on the Grant and I was a short-timer. I further explained my time would run over if I went on this upcoming tour on the Permit. However, I understood a crew member is required to stay behind in the barrack's, assigned to the Master at Arms. He said, "That's correct." I suggested I would volunteer for that duty position until my time was served, which would end in a few months. This would take the burden off of selecting someone from the crew and simplify matters and would satisfy the situation for the both of us. The XO totally agreed with my plan without hesitation; and that's exactly what happened. Up to then, I was sweating bullets. It ended up being a great day. I left the Permit and headed for the beach for a celebration.

Orders were cut which officially transferred me to the sub base barracks as the Permit's permanent duty attendant. Prior to this, I was stuck in limbo. Maybe going to sea, or maybe not. The transfer was a great relief for me. This terrific agreement I cut with the XO, would always make me remember that, "it never hurts to ask." It was a good agreement we accomplished together. No more sea time for me! And even though I loathed being assigned to the sub barracks, it was much nicer than taking another ride to sea. Especially as it was the sister ship of a doomed boat (Thresher). The Permit was later found to have a 51' crack in its pressure hull.

Well, I met with the Master at Arms (my new boss) and he too was easy to get along with. We decided that if I brought him a big bottle of booze, this would shorten my work week to only three hours per day, 8-11am with weekends off. That's only three hours a day. Not even worthwhile showing up for, but I did without hesitation. I didn't want to mess up the good thing. On some evenings I had to return to the base to stand the evening fire watch. I still can't believe the XO went along with my suggestion. It was so pain free for me, and made so much sense for the both of us. Before I knew it, the Permit was returning to sea and I was standing my first fire watch in the barracks. Everything turned out just as I expected and hoped. I interpreted the

XO's decision as a parting gift for me leaving the navy soon. He would have been a great XO serving on the Grant when I was there and my faith in officers could have been restored .

DISCHARGE FROM THE NAVY ~

Discharge day was soon approaching, so I hoped for a local discharge as it would work out better for me to stay here in Hawaii. I predicted a logistic hassle moving to the mainland just to deal with my military discharge. Staying here made better sense. I was already set up with my Seaside Avenue residence. Previously, recent local discharges requests were granted, so I had a good reason to believe I'd be staying here. I didn't want to surrender my cottage, acquaintances, friends, and future possibilities for employment. I had already established the comfort zone that I'd struggled for during my time here.

As things turned out, my luck went south, when I was notified my local discharge was disapproved. I wouldn't be surprised if Mr. Happy played a part in my transfer. I received the disappointing news, which included a transfer to Treasure Island, near San Francisco, instead. Chris got transferred to the U.S.S. Jackson. Their boat was headed for the shipyards at Bremerton, Washington. I held back as long as I could, then reluctantly turned the cottage back to the Islander Hotel. My original roommates had already moved on with new assignments. It was a sad event when I finally returned four sets of keys to the hotel management. For the last few days, I moved into the sub base barracks for the last time. I awaited transfer papers and a plane ride off the island. My seabag was packed and I was ready to fly out the following day.

My last night in Waikiki was at "The Schooner," a place that I occasionally frequented. It was a popular landmark cocktail lounge located on the main strip in Waikiki, a stone's throw to the ocean. A life-size familiar, colorfully painted, wood carving of a Sea Captain stood outside the front door. I was there with a small group of friends attending the last comedy show of the evening. We stayed 'til closing and shut the place down. Throughout the evening, I was exchanging mellow vibes with an attractive nurse who was seated next to me, but not part of our group. It seemed strange that we never shared a word during the entire evening. The place was too loud being seated next to the stage.

When it was time to leave, she took me by the hand and led me outside. We walked 1/2 block before I asked, "Where are we going?" She answered, "we're going to my place." I went along with her sugges- tion. It was an appealing gesture. "Why didn't I think of that?! " I tagged along with little resistance, no arm twisting required. The tropic breeze kept us upright and followed us back during the long walk to her place. I was fully aware I drank too much that evening. Her apartment was located next to the Ilikai Hotel that overlooked the boat harbor. Being with her marked one of the finer evenings of my submarine days here. I carefully explained that I was leaving the island in the morning, but it didn't seem to faze her. She had other plans for me.

It's interesting how life can issue an unexpected set of circum- stances, like being in the wrong place and time, or being in the right place at the right time. In this instance, it was a little of both. It was the right place, but the timing was cut short. Why didn't I meet her earlier when I had more time? She was genuinely warm, intriguing, interesting, and pleasant to be with…maybe, even a keeper. The tim- ing was good in the sense that I got to know her for only a few hours but, also unforgiving in that I was leaving her the following morning.

LOOKING BACK ~

Over the years, I embraced my R&R period like an old friend, as I looked forward to another fresh start, by decluttering my mind and to ditch all that submarine baggage. At the very onset, I left my sailor identity at Ford Island in the search of something better to fill the gap in my lack luster life. I successfully vanished into obscurity as a beach bum in the heart of paradise, never revealing the sailor side of my existence. My interest in the navy faded long ago to discover and reside in the outstanding tourist mecca of Waikiki. When it was time, I saw no incentive to re-up in the navy. I was just biding my time until my enlistment-time ran out. I sensed there was a change coming soon, which would take me away from my place of comfort. The friends, and all the possibilities that could have been, those relationships vanished in a flash. The navy still had a grasp on me, but not for long. Knowing that I wasn't returning, I placed the past behind me. Looking ahead towards tomorrow, casted an eerie outlook of uncertainty. The thought of leaving my sanctuary of comfort, seemed to be unsettling. It was left not knowing what to expect. The year was 1970 and hopes of a brighter future was waiting just ahead somewhere out there.

TREASURE ISLAND ~

I didn't realize it took so long to get discharged from the Navy. I'd been here at Treasure Island for a few days now and there was absolutely zero movement towards getting out. The process needed a laxative boost. The discharge process was drastically slow, with lines of veterans everywhere you looked. It was severely backed up, and Treasure Island was a collection point for the troops from everywhere exiting the Vietnam war.

The system was bogged down with another seemingly disorganized snafu. I'd like to call it a back to back situation of "cluster fucks," one going in and I coming out. It's nothing new, I've run across these navy encounters many times before. Getting released from the navy was equivalent to seeing a doctor at today's hospital emergency rooms, relentlessly impossible. The base was overrun with dischargees, including many from other branches of military service, all gathered here in overwhelming numbers and waiting to go home. Maybe this explains the "120 day early out." They needed the extra time (disguised as an early out) to process me out. I would have been better off staying put where I was, until they really needed me to show up, then transfer me here. I could have used the extra time saying my good-byes to my new nurse, instead of rudely rushing off. The military should have made better use of time. During the year 1970 alone, 100,000 troops were sent home from Vietnam and many showed up here to get discharged.

Any traces of the 1939 Word's Fair at Treasure Island were long gone, just a few buildings remain. Treasure Island (T.I.) is a large man made island, (an attached appendage) of 400 acres, located on the north side of Yerba Buena Island. Both are located in the middle of San Francisco Bay. The island was made for hosting the World's Fair. But now in its place, stood another blighted and abandoned military base, sadly appointed for this inefficient demarcation effort. The base was refitted and brought back to life with temporary processing areas, marked with many structures were scattered throughout the island. Each one required a visit by the outgoing veteran to get signed off. A collection of signatures was necessary before reporting at the main office to plead your case that you were finished with the required paperwork. The slowness of getting something done reminded me of a slow motion "deja vu" version of a lengthy submarine patrol of never ending. This equates to many hours of standing in lengthy lines. There's no order. Just choose a line and stand there.

Barracks and chow halls were scattered throughout the base. If you went to eat at the chow hall or to take a squirt, you would risk losing your place in line for discharge. This explains all the vending machines conveniently located everywhere.

Your days were spent as a permanent fixture in endless lines. This led you to wondered, Why the delay? Your paperwork might have been misplaced in the stacks of paper; or worse, lost in the shuffle. And the time wasted standing around was a slow tease. The only rush here was the one created in your own mind. The process was the final test of anyone's patience. "Focus on relaxing and go with the flow." I kept telling myself, "I'm getting out soon," and the end is somewhere out there.

During the wait, volumes of paperwork needed to be processed for each departing veteran. This included getting issued a departing paycheck, a physical examination if needed, a review list of your previous duty stations, a complete compendium of your military career. It was a list of reminders you'd forgotten over the years. Above all, was the importance of the DD214, the proof of service document. It had more value than the final paycheck. It contained the proof of military service including the history of each G.I.'s military career, a great document for finding employment on the outside. The honorable discharge document and pin were also issued.

In the main office of the base you could hear the clatter of typewriters moving at warp speed. You can almost sense the heat rising off them as they keep pace with the waiting lines. Buildings spread throughout the multiple acre site were turned into make-shift doctors offices, dental offices, eyes, ears and throat, and other medical inspection stations; and were crammed to the max accommodating the outflow of veterans. Treasure Island was the last point in dealing with hundreds of early-out military personnel. Now, I understood why my local discharge request went bust. Pearl Harbor couldn't handle processing a high number of vets. The hurry-up to get here created more confusion for everyone arriving here at Treasure Island. Timing of the movement could have been more evenly spread throughout the calendar year, in order to ease the "discharge turmoil." The discharge process seemingly forgot to match the in-flow numbers with the outflow numbers, that caused the backlog of troops. I was part of the outflow along with everyone else, and impatience was heard in the ranks. The time delay was an unexpected interference that neutralized the 120 day early-out. It was looking more like a wicked snafu for the vets as the supposedly smooth exit process was backfiring. Hopefully, this was the last military boondoggle I would ever witness.

THE END IS NEAR ~

Eating lunch in the mess hall after assembling all my paperwork, I happened to spot a familiar face from the Grant. It was my friend John Lemieux pulling a shift in the mess hall. During his break, we discovered we were getting discharged about a week apart. It was coincidental we were both from Sacramento. With no pressing agenda on our schedules, we planned to move to Reno and find work in the casinos for a fresh start. It was great to be permanently separated from the Navy. I never looked back. After the dust settled, I had a paltry sum of $800 to my name, including my final paycheck. That's not much to show for the four years, but at this point it really didn't matter. I was headed for Reno, where fun and excitement awaits me.

I was twenty-five years old when I walked out the front gate at Treasure Island. My long four year navy life was finally over. But, those years were still imbedded in my memory. I caught a ride with an old friend back home. Home to Sacramento for a brief visit before heading to Reno. Guess who picked me up? I would have remained in Hawaii if I'd received that local discharge. As it turned out, getting sent to Treasure Island to be discharged ended all possibilities of returning to paradise.

It was interesting living in Waikiki in the 1960's. I noticed a gradual transitional change in my surroundings each time I took my R&R. But at one point, there was a flood of changes that swept the Islands. Accompanying those changes, came the Beatles invasion, psychedelic trends, the hippie revolution, weird music, and potheads. Tourists and co-eds arrived as visitors, but soon after, an onslaught of many of them arrived from the United States, Canada, and Japan. Some moved in, seeking permanent residency. Waikiki became an international blend of cultures, attitudes, influences, and different points of view. Changes were both good and bad. Rock'n roll music was the good part. Not so much the drugs that followed alongside.

Unfortunately, they both became inseparable. I learned of the changes when I returned from my patrol at sea.

Living in Paradise was an enjoyable and unique experience, even through the hard times of frugality. It offered a sense of belonging and connection with the revolving events of the time. Life in Waikiki was the heartbeat and centerpiece of my journey. As a young sailor during the Vietnam war, I couldn't have landed a better assignment for military duty. Since my departure, I've kept in touch with my close friends Chris Wenzl and John Lemieux. I smile thinking of the good times that we shared some 50 years ago.

Looking back at my four years in the Navy were quite a puzzling contradiction of time. Although time passed by fairly quickly, it seemed those five patrols on the Grant were anchored in time, a bothersome turn of a never ending story that goes on much the same today as it did then...... "rats in a can" under an endless abyss.

Memories are fleeting flashes from the past.
They cross your mind, then suddenly vanish.
Hopefully you found this submarine voyage thoroughly
insightful as I did writing it.
Bon Voyage ~

GLOSSARY ~ *submarine abbreviations, terms and meaning.*

AMC Automatic Maneuvering Control. Auto Control for the Planesman.

BCP Ballast Control Panel (Operator) Controls depth and trim of submarine while on patrol.

DINK Sailor delinquent in Sub qualifications.

FBM Fleet Ballistic Missile Submarine. (Nuclear powered w/16 nuclear missiles).

LLOPS Lower Level Operations Compartment.

MCC Missile Control Center

MASTER AT ARMS A position of authority, such as the barracks or another designated area.

1MC Emergency announcements to the Control Room, Captain's quarters and to Maneuvering. Given from different stations within the boat.

MANEUVERING The engineering space(back-aft) that controls the sub's nuclear propulsion.

NON-QUAL Any crew member not qualified in submarines.

OD (Officer of the Deck) in charge of the Control Room and sub operations during the shift.

PLANESMEN Driver of the Boat.

R&R Rest and Relaxation. Time off, in between patrols. The third R meaning: Recovery.

SHIT-STIRRERS Trouble makers, pranksters, those who operate surreptitiously.

SUBMARINE Sub, Boat, FBM, Boomer.

SUB QUALS A comprehensive and rigorous course in submarine qualifications.

TRIM Balance point of the sub. Control of Sub's attitude: side to side and teeter-toddler type.

TDU Trash Disposal Unit. A vertical tube that hold cylindrical cans of trash to be shot to sea.

XO Executive Officer, senior position just below the Captain of the Boat.

ABOUT THE AUTHOR ~

According to others, I appear younger than my 72 years; but everyone knows you can't judge a book from its cover. Looking beyond the exterior shell, tells a much different story. I am basically a physical wreck after enduring two heart surgeries, complications from diabetes, bone on bone hips, pains from arthritis, and increasing blurry vision. Having consumed 27 tons of red meat over the years, is the most-likely reason for my current condition. These ailments could be easily blamed my 26 years working in the Sacramento Fire Department; but I won't. That's too easy.

Working as a Fireman and then as a Fire Investigator for many years, you're bound to catch something. I escaped catching fire, but I caught all the other nasty stuff instead. That comes with the territory. Why complain? We all catch something during the aging process. I have caught more than my fair share. I see it as a good thing, that is, taking a hit for the team, the "team of aging."

Looking at the number of prescription drugs I ingest every day, I wonder what will I catch next? If I put them all in a bowl and cover them with skim-milk, it could pass as new-heart-healthy breakfast cereal. Yum. I wonder if this qualifies for taking my meds with food? I can only guess how many calories are in this mystery blend of healing. I was asked by my doctor to lose a few pounds. I am currently working on that. I need all the improvement that I can muster up, to live life to its fullest; and escape living life in the shortest life span.

Two years ago, I decided to write this book. Everyone has a book somewhere inside them; you just need grab those thoughts and put it on paper. My book came as a gnawing reminder from the past; and it became apparent to me that it was something that I needed to deal with. I moved on from telling stories to writing stories. I hope you enjoy the book. It is written for the lay person; and, men and women alike seem to take to it. This is my version of what occurred during the narrow time frame in the second half of the 1960s while serving on the U.S.S. U.S. Grant. My saga is told as a personal tour while serving on this submarine; picture yourself right beside me, as I tell many contrasting stories during my Rest & Relaxation (R&R) periods. I am your personal submarine tour guide.

Today, I'm just a retired "FireBum" lounging outdoors by a swimming pool. I found my new paradise. It's considered a new found therapy, making-up for those lost years of submarine time.

Additional copies can be purchased directly
through Amazon.com

57518716R00117

Made in the USA
San Bernardino, CA
21 November 2017